PREFACE

Slang is an integral part of any language. Every country, no matter what language they speak, has a unique slang. Even if you have studied a particular language, you'll have a hard time understanding the slang that is used in the country where that language is spoken, or maybe even the slang of a region inside that country.

I have been teaching Spanish online for more than 3 years, and while talking to my students, I've noticed how interested they were in learning "mexislang."

They asked me about it all the time, and it started to fascinate me as well. I realized how slang didn't follow any rules and was constantly changing, day by day.

I created a blog where I started posting entries for my students, to better explain them how slang words were used and why.

These blog posts have evolved into this book.

Here, I gather the most important phrases and words of mexislang and explain their history and usage, including examples.

You will find this manual useful if...

- you want to learn Spanish from Mexico;
- you are going to travel to Mexico;
- you want to understand Mexican culture better;
- you like learning new languages;
- you want to communicate better with Mexican people;

- you want to learn the most recent Mexican slang (and internet slang), from 2018;
- You want to learn slang from a real Mexican tutor who has taught Spanish to people from all around the world.

Mexico is the 8th most visited country in the world, and #1 in Latin America, so this is a book that can be used by adventurers, businessmen, spring breakers, and any average joe who wants to make bonds, communicate, and establish good relationships with Mexican people.

Before going to the actual meat of this manual, I want to thank every single person who has helped me on the journey of writing my very first book, especially because I happened to write it in a language that isn't even my native tongue.

I would like to start with my friend Felipe Vasconcelos, who is a freelance illustrator and the artist responsible for the cover art of this book. You can check more of his work at www.felvast.com. If you choose to hire him for your own projects, I can assure you he'll do a fantastic job, for very accessible prices.

Also, I want to thank Felipe's girlfriend, Gabriela Azuara, who helped me set up my blog, and gave me a lot of support throughout my writing. She knows how to motivate people by making them realize what they are capable of.

To Emanuel Vasconcelos, Felipe's brother, and Juliana Benavides, a freelancer from Venezuela, who proofread and edited the whole book.

MEXISLANG   RAÚL JIMÉNEZ

To my friend Chris from Greece, who also offered me technical and graphic design guidance.

To every single one of my students. I started my blog for them, but I want to make a special mention to Paul Grillos, and Gabe Wyner, who gave me constant support and good advice while I was writing.

To my muse, Zari Akkuly, who gave me motivation and inspiration. Her support helped me go on through all the hardships I had to endure to finish this book.

To my parents who have let me live in their house for all these years, and have always given me everything I needed without ever asking for anything in return.

And lastly, to all my friends here in Mexico, as well as every single person who helped me in my research for words and expressions.

There's too many of them to name everyone, but everything that's awesome about this book, is thanks to them. On the other hand, everything that is not so awesome is completely my fault.

Thanks to everyone for all your help and support!

Disclaimer

First and foremost, while all the words and expressions in this book are informal, a lot of them are used in a current basis even in formal events, and by powerful and educated people. Even so, I don't recommend using most of them with people who are in a higher hierarchy than you (e.g. your boss), or people who are not friends with you yet. You will have to use them at your own risk, or you can warn everyone beforehand that your Spanish isn't 100% perfect so that you can prevent any misunderstandings.

Also, Mexican culture has always been kind of misogynistic and homophobic; so many words can be offensive to certain groups, like women and people from the LGBT community. Those offensive words figure here because they are part of the dialect, and it's necessary to know them to fully understand it better. In any case, the author doesn't condone the harmful use of these words against anyone; they are explained purely for educational purposes.

Table of Contents

Chapter 1 1

The Most Used Mexislang Words 1

   Chingar 1

   Madre 5

   Pinche 10

   PEDO 10

   Verga 12

   Güey 15

   Cagar 15

   Puto 16

   No manches 18

   Mamar 19

   Cabrón 21

   Coger 21

   Mierda 22

   Chido 23

   Chale 23

   Huevo 24

   Culo 25

Pendejo 26

Chapter 2 27

Internet Slang...27

   Character archetypes. 27

   Mirrey 27

   Lobuki...28

   Luchona 28

   Bendición 29

   Mañoso/Narco 29

   Buchón 29

   BUCHÓN LANGUAGE...31

   Fierro..31

   Pariente..31

   Arre 31

   Viejón 32

   Encobijado..32

   Levantón 32

   Niño rata 32

   LANGUAGE OF RAT KIDS (Modern geeky internet slang) 33

   Arenoso..33

   Ap 33

Elfa 33

Lince 33

Me encorazona 34

Me emputa / me emperra 34

Me enflorece 34

Me enjotece / me enjota / me enmaricona 34

Laura sad 34

El Zelda 34

La dvd 34

Repollo /repoio /rechicken 35

Chidori/shidori 35

Virgo 35

Ward 35

Pack 35

Papu/Perro/Perrazo 35

Nepe 35

Momo 35

Momazo 35

Naik 36

Gfa 36

Chairo 36

- Únicas y diferentes 36
- Nini 37
- Juniors 37
- Ladys and lords 38
- Cholo 38
- Don vergas 38
- Godínez 39
- Fifí 39

Chapter 3 40
MexiSayings and Expressions 40
- Taparle el ojo al macho 40
- Hacerse pato 40
- Sacar la sopa 41
- ¿Nos peinamos o nos hacemos trenzas? 41
- En menos de lo que canta un gallo 42
- En corto 42
- Ser un estuche de monerías 43
- Atáscate que hay lodo 43
- Por si las moscas 44
- Ser ajonjolí de todos los moles 44
- Hacer changuitos 45

Echarle mucha crema a tus tacos 45

Planchar oreja 45

Oir pasos en la azotea 46

El que es perico donde quiera es verde 46

Vamos a ver de qué lado masca la iguana 47

Estar como agua para chocolate 47

Es puro pájaro nalgón 48

Me cae / Me cae bien / Me cae mal 48

Brincos dieras 49

Echarse su taco 49

El horno no está para los bollos 50

Por detroit 50

Estar cura 51

De chocolate 51

Dar atole con el dedo 52

Me late 52

Ser cuchillito de palo 53

Bajar avión 53

Dar el avión 54

Ser concha 54

¿Y tu nieve de que la quieres? 55

- Sin chiste 55
- Echar la firma 56
- ¿A qué hora sales por el pan? 56
- De a grapa 57
- Alborotar el gallinero 57
- Aquí nada más mis chicharrones truenan 58
- A caballo regalado no se le ve el diente 58
- Está cañón 58
- No dar paso sin huarache 59
- Ya salió el peine 59
- Traer el Jesús en la boca 60
- Me hace lo que el viento a Juárez 60
- Dar el gatazo 61
- Dar el rol 61
- Pasarse de tueste 61
- Hacer un pancho 62
- No pega ni con chicle 62
- Colgar los tenis 63
- Di rana y yo salto 63
- Ya rugiste 63
- Agarrar de su puerquito 64

- Hablando del rey de Roma...65
- Mal del Puerco 65
- Ya te cargó el payaso 65
- Barajéamela más despacio...66
- No cantas mal las rancheras 67
- Andar pariendo cuates...67
- Ir a mi arbolito..68
- Hacer del uno / Hacer del dos..68
- Comerse la torta antes del recreo..68
- Dar una mochada 69
- Ponerse la del puebla 69
- Ponerse las pilas 70
- Caer gordo..70
- Estar salado 71
- Mame / El tren del mame 71
- Sacar canas verdes 72
- No tener pelos en la lengua 72
- Pegarle al gordo 73
- Al chile...73
- Sana, sana, colita de rana...74
- La venganza de Moctezuma...74

- Caerte el veinte 75
- Te hace falta barrio 76
- Tener el nopal en la cara 76
- Buena onda/mala onda/ ¿qué onda? 76
- De tín, Marin 78
- De pelos 78
- Dar lata 78
- De panzaso 79
- Manita de gato 79
- Media naranja 79
- La pinta 80

Chapter 4 80
Mexislang verbs 80

- Pichicatear 80
- Chiflar 81
- Bacilar 81
- Apañar 81
- Mear 82
- Pichar 82
- Ningunear 82
- Chamaquear 83

Amolarse	83
Bajar	84
Paletear	84
Balconear	85
Batear	85
Terapear	86
Sangrar	86
Cantinflear	86
Jinetear	87
Catafixiar	87
Pelar	88
Pelarse	88
Pelársela	89
Que alguien te la pele	89
Rajar	89
Rajarse	90
Guacarearse	90
Chulear	90
Bañársela	91
Castrar	91
Pandear	92

- Sordear 92
- Jalar 93
- Machetear 93

Chapter 5 94
Mexislang words 94
- Chafa 94
- Gringo 95
- Chavo/Morro/Ruco 96
- Gato 97
- Fresa 98
- Naco 98
- ¡Aguas! 99
- Aza/Azo/Ala 99
- Chamba 100
- Carnal 101
- Chesco 101
- Lana/varo/feria 102
- Hueva 102
- Vato 103
- Orale 103
- Ules, Oles, Eles and Ales 105

Malinchista 107

Bronca 108

Paro 108

Tianguis 109

Neta 110

Jefe/Jefa 110

Reta 110

Troca 111

Cantón 111

Cuate 111

Canijo 112

Gacho 112

Ardido 113

Ratero 113

Chilango 114

Codo 114

Guácala 115

Betabel 115

Vago 115

Coyote 116

Fusca 116

- Mamache 117
- Pata 117
- Ñoño 117
- Mordida 118
- Tocayo 118
- Piocha 118
- Mojón 119
- Jeta 119
- Chompa 119
- Plomazo 120
- Gandalla 120
- Machín 120
- Cascarita 121
- Mojado 121
- Pollero 122
- Simón 122
- Nel 123
- Chacha 123
- Fulano/Fulana 124
- Barco 124
- Guachicol 125

- Cariñoso 125
- Baboso 126
- Matado 126
- La banda 126
- Cachirul 127
- Sobres 127
- Aventón 127
- Chingaquedito 128
- Sangrón 128
- Agüitarse 129
- Chilpayate 129
- Palanca 129
- Chiripa 130
- Argüende 130
- Perro 131
- Federal 132
- Entenado 132
- Mirruña 133
- El bote 133
- Piñas 133
- Llevado 134

Chivas 134

El sope 135

Cursi 135

Zafo 135

Acordeón 136

Trucha 136

Pelado 136

Gallo 137

Guapachoso 138

Puñetas 138

Pitero 139

Mono 139

Ñero 140

Barbero 140

Alcahuete 140

Tronco 141

Vientos 141

Cámara 142

Cafre 142

Fantoche 142

Valedor 143

- Fritangas 143
- Chucherías 143
- Garnachas 144
- Chamuco 144
- Chicano 144
- Botana 145
- Chengo 145
- Chitón 145
- Prieto 146
- Greña 146
- Sobaco 146
- Matasanos 147
- Guarura 147
- Equis 147
- Todólogo: 148
- Choninos/chones: 148

Chapter 6 149
Party, drugs and alcohol Mexislang words. 149
- Antro 149
- Perreo 149
- Rola 150

- Cotorrear ... 151
- Chela ... 151
- Caguama ... 152
- Agualoca ... 152
- Pistear ... 153
- Pomo ... 153
- Mala copa ... 154
- Estar fumado ... 154
- Mota ... 155
- Churro ... 155
- Tachas ... 156
- Perico ... 157
- Cruda ... 157
- Quinceañera ... 157
- Chambelán ... 158

Chapter 7 ... 159
Sex, sexuality and dating Mexislang words ... 159
- Mexislang ways to say penis ... 159
- Mexislang ways to say vagina ... 160
- Mexislang ways to say breasts ... 161
- Mexislang ways to say testicles ... 162

- Mexislang ways to refer to homosexuals ... 162
- Mexislang ways to say semen ... 163
- Bajarse por los chescos ... 164
- Un mameluco ... 164
- Empiernarse ... 164
- Apapacho ... 165
- Pechugona ... 165
- Orto ... 166
- Darle vuelo a la hilacha. ... 166
- Jalársela ... 166
- Manuela ... 167
- Ser una nalga ... 167
- La regla ... 168
- Tirar aceite ... 168
- Deslecharse ... 169
- Tronar el ejote ... 169
- Ponedor(a) ... 169
- Apretada ... 170
- Gordibuena(o) ... 170
- Pedorro ... 170
- Trapo ... 171

- Estar Carita 171
- La jarocha 172
- Piruja 172
- Piropo 172
- Mi Viejo / Vieja 173
- Tener pegue 173
- Taco de ojo 174
- Aflojar 174
- Fajar 175
- Putero 175
- Echarse un palo 176
- Chacalón(a) 176
- Mayate 176
- Cornudo 177
- Sancho 177
- Teibol 178
- Ligar 178
- Estar Bueno(a) 178
- Albur 179
- Hacer de chivo los tamales 180
- Tirar rollo 180

Echar los perros	181
Viejo rabo verde	181
Mandilón	181
Panochón	182
Toloache	183
Encueros	183
Cachondo	184
Piojito	184
Hermanos de leche	184
Ganado	185
Immerse in the language:	186
Some ways to improve your Spanish	186

Chapter 1
The Most Used Mexislang Words

This is the first time in my life that I have undertaken a task as big and intimidating as writing a book in a foreign language. Right now, as I write this, I'm also trying to categorize the 400+ words and expressions I have collected over the years. It's quite hard for me to sort them into categories.

This is because Mexican lingo has words with a lot of meanings depending on the context, and there are many words and expressions that share the same meaning, but also have a few multiple meanings depending on the situation they are being used in.

So, this first chapter is going to be composed of all of those words and phrases that are, in my own opinion, used the most in Mexican slang.

Chingar

Chingar is probably the most used verb in Mexican slang. You'll hear it a lot and quite consistently across the whole country, but it has a bit of a history to it.

Some people refer to Mexicans as "*hijos de la chingada*", which literally means, "sons of the *chingada*". This is because native Latin American women were raped by Spanish colonizers. So, you can say they were *chingadas* by them.

As you may have deduced already, one of the many meanings of *chingar*, is to rape or to have sex, more specifically, vapid sex. It's mostly used when a man is being a jerk and brags to his friends about that one time he had sex with a lady just for fun and without any romantic intentions.

Chingar is a violent verb most of the times. When you say things like "*chinga tu madre*" (Fuck your mother) or "*¡Vete a chingar a otro lado!*" (Get the fuck away from me), you are literally throwing Mexican F-bombs, but besides being a Mexican equivalent of the F-word, *chingar* can have a lot of meanings, depending on the context.

1.- Most of the times, *chingar* means to annoy someone. You can also use the verb *joder* for this, but *chingar* is more common in Mexico.

Ex:

¡No estés chingando!	Cut it out!
¡Cómo chingas!	Damn you're annoying!

2.- *Chingar* can also be used to say something broke, or is not working. *Joder* also works the same way for this use.

Ex.

Esto se chingó.	This thing broke/This thing stopped working.

Eso está chingado. That thing doesn't work.

3.-*Chingar* can also be used when you are going to screw someone up, mainly in a physical fight. *Verguear*, *putear*, and *madrear* (Words that come from *verga*, *puto* and *madre*) serve for the exact same meaning.

The main difference is that while those three work only for screwing over someone physically, *chingar* can also mean to harm someone by lying to them, or taking advantage of people, besides physical harm. You can also use *joder*, exactly as *chingar* for this meaning.

Ex.

¡Te voy a chingar! I'm going to bust your ass!

¡Te dejaron bien chingado! They beat you up pretty bad.

4.- You can modify *chingar* (verb) and make it into *chingón* (adjective), which is the mexislang equivalent of badass.

Ex.

Que chingón está este libro. This book is pretty badass.

5.- To express you have a lot of something, you change *chingar (verb)* into *chingo*, or *chingazo (quantifiers)*.

Tengo un chingo de hambre. I'm fucking starving.

Tengo un chingazo de libros. I have a shitload of books.

6.- To consume things such as food, drinks, entertainment, etc.

Ex.

Ayer me chingué veinte tacos. I ate twenty tacos yesterday.

Me voy a chingar unas cheves. I'm going to drink some beers.

Me chingué todos los westerns de Sergio Leone el fin de semana. I binge watched all of Sergio Leone's westerns during the weekend.

7.- To refer to a physical hit, or a fist punch, you change *chingar* (verb) into *chingazo*, or *chingadazo* (nouns). The words *madrazo*, *vergazo*, and *putazo*, mean exactly the same.

Ex.

Me di un chingazo en la cabeza cuando me levanté de la cama. I hit my head when I rose from bed.

8.- You can make *chingar* (verb) into *chingaderas* (noun), and you use it when you want to refer to unwanted objects, or sometimes, even silly, idiotic or pointless things.

Ex.

Dame esa chingadera. — Give me that fucking thing.

Deberías estar trabajando en vez de andar viendo chingaderas. — You should be working instead of watching pointless stuff.

Madre

Madre, which means mother, is a word used a lot in Mexican slang, mostly to accentuate other words and sentences, and give them more power and importance. Here is a compilation of examples with their own explanations of some expressions using *madre*.

Desmadre:

It means making or being a mess. As a verb, *desmadrar,* it can also mean to destroy something. People also use the word "*desvergue*" and "*despapaye*" in the same context.

Ex.

Desmadraste mi casa cuando te la presté. — You destroyed my house when I lend it to you.

El huracán hizo de este barrio un desmadre. — The hurricane made this neighborhood a mess.

Eres un desmadre. — You are a pretty fucked up dude (like in a fun-loving kind of way)

Poca madre/a toda madre/con madre

It means very cool, or very nice.

Ex.

Este nuevo videojuego está poca madre. This new videogame is very cool.

De a madre

Same as *un chingo*, it means a lot and it's used as a quantifier.

Ex.

Tengo de a madre de problemas. I have a lot of problems.

A raja madre /hecho madres

Sometimes "raja puta", or only "a raja", it means doing something, or going very fast.

Ex.

Ten cuidado. En esa autopista hay muchos accidentes porque los autos van a raja madre / Be careful. In that freeway there's a lot of accidents, because people drive like *hechos madre.* crazy.

Chingada madre

Dammit, or goddammit.

Ex.

Chingada madre. Todo salió mal. Damn it! Everything went to shit!

Chinga tu madre

Literally "Fuck your mother" but it's actually used as a way of saying "Go fuck yourself" or just "Fuck you".

Ex.

Te odio. Chinga tu madre. I hate you. Fuck your mother.

Chingar la madre

To be annoying and bother someone.

Ex.

Ya deja de chingar la madre. Stop busting my balls.

Chingue su madre

"fuck it", like when you get bold, and you decide to do something without hesitation or concern for the consequences.

Ex.

Chingue su madre. No voy a ir al trabajo mañana. Quiero salir de fiesta hoy hasta tarde.

Fuck it. I'm not going to work tomorrow. I wanna party until late tonight.

Esa/esta/aquella madre:

That, these/those thing(s). People tend to also use esa/esta/aquella mierda or verga, to talk about things.

Ex.

Pásame esa madre.

Pass me that thing.

Mentar madres:

To swear.

Ex.

Creo que estaba encabronado, porque se la pasó mentando madres todo el rato.

I think he was pissed off, because he was swearing all the time.

Valer madre

Sucking at doing something. This is a very interesting phrase because both *"valer madre"*, and *"no valer madre"* mean the same, negative thing: Being terrible at something. People also use *"no vales verga"* as the exact same thing.

Ex.

No vales madre jugando futbol.   You suck at playing soccer.

Me vale madre

I don't give a damn.

Ex.

Vas a lastimar al perrito.   You are going to hurt the doggy.

– Me vale madre el pinche perrito.   – I don't give a damn about the fucking doggy.

Romper/partir la madre.

It means to harm someone physically and beat the crap out of him.

Ex.

Ese cabrón le rompio/partió la madre a mi amigo.   That asshole beat the crap out of my friend.

Madrazo: A physical hit or fist punch.

Ex.

Qué buenos madrazos da ese boxeador.   That boxer throws great punches.

Pinche

The original meaning of *pinche* is actually "kitchen helper", but in Mexislang, you use it when you want to accentuate something, or when you want to say: "this damn thing".

If the adjective you are using it with is negative, or offensive in any way, it can become way more offensive, because of its emphatic nature, instead of "this damn thing" it'll become more like a "this fucking something".

Ex.

Pinche ratero.   Fucking thief.

Moscú es muy bonito, pero que pinche frío hace aquí.   Moscow is very pretty, but what damn cold there is here.

PEDO

Pedo could be noun or an adjective and it literally means "fart", but it has many meanings depending on the context.

1.- You use *pedo* to say you are drunk, or you really like to get drunk.

Ex.

Ando bien pedo. I'm wasted.

Somos bien pedotes. We really like to get drunk.

2.- When there's a party, and there will be a lot of alcohol in that party.

Ex.

Vamos a hacer una peda. Let's make a party. (with alcohol)

3.- To say something is a lie you use "*puro pedo*", to say someone is a liar, you use "*pedero*".

Ex.

No creas todo lo que lees en internet. Esa noticia es puro pedo. Don't believe everything you read on the internet. Those news are bullshit.

No le creas a ese güey. Es un pedero. Don't believe that guy. He is a bullshitter.

4.- To talk about problems.

Ex.

Ven a mi fiesta. No hay pedo si Come to my party. It's no

no tienes dinero.	problem if you don't have money.
Tengo muchos pedos con mi esposa.	I have a lot of problems with my wife.

5.- To say "what's up?" to a close friend.

Ex.

¿Qué pedo güey?	What's up dude?

6.- To express fear, you say "sacar un pedo".

Ex.

Me sacaste un pedo.	You scared the crap out of me.

Verga

According to dictionaries, the word *verga* refers to either the highest pole on a ship, or the masculine genitalia. You can guess which meaning is the most used in Mexican slang. It's literally the equivalent of dick and/or cock, but as always, the language has given the word different meanings depending on the context. Also, *verga* is probably one of the harshest words in Mexican slang. People cannot even say it on rated-R TV.

MEXISLANG

1.- To express something kicks ass.

¿Escuchaste esa canción?	Did you hear that song?
Si, está muy verga.	Yeah, it kicks ass.

2.- Referring to a beat up or punches.

Se verguearon al boxeador en la pelea.	The boxer had his ass handed to him in the fight.
Le dio un vergazo en la cara.	He punched him hard in the face.

The words *putazo* or *madrazo* also work the same way and they mean "a punch" in Mexican slang.

3.-Sending someone to fuck himself.

Vete a la verga.	Go fuck yourself.

For this one, people often also use the word "*chingada*", instead of "*verga*". Both are hypothetical places that are very far away, so the meaning is the same.

4.- When someone thinks too much of himself.

Se cree muy verga.	He thinks he is the real deal.

5.- Talking about something you don't know, or being derogatory about it.

¿Qué es esa verga?	What the hell is that shit?

In this last use, other words can be used instead, and have the exact same derogatory meaning, like *madre*, *mierda*, etc.

6.- You use "no valer verga" to express that something isn't very good or of bad quality. You can also use, *madre* or *cabeza*, instead of *verga* to express the same.

Este auto no vale verga.	This car sucks.
Este auto vale verga.	This car sucks.

7.- When you have a lot of things, or when you want to accentuate something, you say *un vergo* or un *vergazo* (quantifiers).

Example:

Hace un vergo de frío.	It's fucking freezing.
Tengo un vergazo de dinero.	I have a shitload of money.

8.- To express fear or surprise.

Example:

¡¡Verga!! Me sacaste un pedote.	Damn! You scared the shit out of me.

Güey

This word comes from a deformation of the word "*buey*" (Ox), and it just means "dude" in Mexico. It's used everywhere and by almost everyone, no matter age, gender or social status, but mostly with close friends.

There are also many words that are used for the exact same thing, like *cabrón*, *puto*, *vato*, *entenado*, *machín*, etc. But most of them are words that are offensive when not used with very close **friends**, and no matter what, *güey* is still the main word used in Mexislang for saying "dude".

Cagar

While *cagar* literally means "taking a shit", it has an array of meanings depending on how it's used.

1.- Hating, disliking or being angry about something.

Me caga la cebolla.	I don't like onion.
Estoy cagado por el calor.	I'm angry because the weather is very hot.

2- Looking very similar to someone else.

Estás cagado a Justin Bieber.   You look just like Justin Bieber.

3.- To say something is very funny.

Están cagados los chistes de ese comediante.   The jokes of that comedian are very funny.

4.- To talk about scolding or nagging someone.

Si mi madre nos descubre, me va a cagar. | If my mother finds out, she'll nag me.

Me cagaron cuando llegué tarde a clase. | I was scolded when I got late to my class.

5.- When someone screws up or fails at something.

La cagué al preparar esta receta, sabe horrible. | I screwed up at making this recipe. It tastes horrible.

No hagas eso. ¡La cagas! | Don't do that. You are screwing it up!

6.- To express extreme fear, as *"me cagué"*. It's an equivalent of shitting my pants.

Me cagué de miedo con esa película. | I got scared as hell with that movie.

Puto

Puto is a pretty popular word. If you like soccer, and have seen the Mexican national team play, you can hear the cheering fans shouting "puuuuuuto" everytime there's a goal kick from the opposite team. What *puto* really means is "faggot", but it's almost never used with homophobic purposes.

The feminine version of this word, *puta*, acquires a different meaning. This is one of the most offensive things that you can say to a woman because it literally means slut or whore.

Getting back to *puto*, its use is extremely diverse and sometimes, even non-sensical. Sometimes we call our best friend *puto* in a sort of loving way. We call *puto* to somone who has stolen from us. We yell "puto" to someone who makes us mad. We make fun of someone who is scared of something, by calling him *puto*. We even laugh at ourselves and say we we're very "*putos*" because we didn't have enough courage to do something. There's a famous song by the Mexican band Molotov called "Puto".

Puto is used daily, and it means whatever the Mexicans want it to mean. Here, everybody is a *puto* from time to time, and there's no escape from it. It's part of the culture. Even if you don't notice it, in Mexico, someone may call you *puto* in his mind at least a few times a day, and I wrote this for you to understand that there is nothing wrong with it because 90% of the times, it's not used with homophobic purposes.

As the memes say, we are so respectful that we call everyone puto (or equivalent words), except the folks who actually are putos.

Ex:

La puta vida.	This damn life.
¿Qué pedo, puto?	What's up dude (to a very close friend)

No se subió a la montaña rusa por puto. He didn't go on the rollercoaster, because he was afraid.

No manches

No manches is a very common phrase used by young people. It's usually used to express surprise, skepticism or discomfort, depending on the context. Other phrases used in the exact same fashion are: *No mames, no jodas, no chingues*. But those are stronger, and must be used mostly around friends, while *no manches* is more socially acceptable, but still informal.

Ex.

¿Quieres aguacate? Do you want some avocado?

- No manches, no me gusta. No manches (discomfort), I don't like it.

Te compré un regalo. I bought you a gift.

-No manches, muchas gracias. No manches (surprise), thanks a lot.

Dicen que los tacos de ese restaurant son los mejores de México. They say the tacos of that restaurant, are the best of all México.

— No manches, los mejores tacos los venden en la calle. No manches! (skepticism) The best tacos are sold on the streets.

Mamar

Mamar literally means to suck something, but besides that, it has many meanings depending on how it's conjugated, or if it's used as a noun.

1.- To say someone is very strong, or has huge muscles, you turn *mamar* into the adjective "*mamado*":

Ex.

Tu amigo está bien mamado. Your friend is very strong.

2.-The word "*mamada*" could mean blowjob, nonsense or bullshit, depending on the context.

Ex.

"*¿Te gustó la película?* Did you like the movie?

No, era una mamada. No, it was a bunch of nonsense.

3.- You can use the verb *mamar*, just as you use *chingar*, to express someone is annoying, or infuriating because of how constantly he keeps doing something that causes discomfort to you or others.

Ex.

Deja de mamar. Knock it off.

No estés mamando. Don't be so pushy – Don't be so annoying.

4.- As a noun *mamón* means asshole. But it can also be used in the expression *"no seas mamón"* to express surprise or disbelief.

Ex.

Es bien mamón. No quiso ayudarme con mi tarea. He is an asshole. He didn't help me with my homework.

5.- *Mamar* when used in the phrase *"te mamaste"* (literally sucking yourself), means that someone went too far with something, like a mean joke or when someone exceeds expectations, or when someone said something very funny.

Ex.

Te la mamaste con este trabajo. You made an outstanding job (it can also mean, making a terrible job, but it depends on context, voice tone, etc.)

-*Se pintó el pelo, no me gustó y la corté.* -She dyed her hair, I didn't like it, so I broke up with her.

-*Te la mamaste.* -You went too fucking far.

6.- You can use *"no mames"* exactly like no manches, but it's stronger, and more informal. Of course, it's something you won't say in front of your mother-in-law when you first meet her, but it's commonly used around friends.

Cabrón

The word *cabra* refers to a female goat, and the word *cabrón*, to the male. In the world of **mexislang**, we call *cabrón*, or *cabrona* to someone who is very tough or skillfull at something, or as a stronger replacement for *güey* with close friends. It also can mean that someone is an *asshole* or a dick.

Ex.

Ganamos porque somos bien cabrones.	We won because we kick ass.
¿Qué pedo, cabrón?	What's up dude? (to a close friend)
Ese cabrón me cobró caro, y ni siquiera hizo un buen trabajo.	That asshole charged me a lot, and he didn't even do a good job.

Coger

This is a very important word to be aware of. In Latin America, it's the slang word that we use to refer to sexual intercourse and we exclusively use it for that. It's an extremely harsh word *and* along with *verga*, *coger* is also another word that people cannot even use in rated-R TV.

However, in Spain, *coger* is a completely normal and inoffensive verb which only means "to grab or to take something".

If you learned Spanish in Spain, and you use the verb *coger* often when you want to say "to *grab*", be very careful when you come to Mexico. If you use that verb, people are going to look at you weird. It's a better idea to stick with the verb *agarrar* which is the actual way that we say "to grab" in Mexico. Always *agarrar*, never *coger*.

Words like *cochar*, *tirar*, *zingar*, *follar* and *joder* also refer to having sex, but are used less in Mexico.

Ex.

Vamos a coger.   Let's fuck.

Mierda

Mierda is the Mexislang equivalent of the word shit. It's almost always used in derogatory ways, to compare people or things with feces, or to say something isn't cool, but *sometimes* it's just used to refer to random stuff and objects, without any bad intentions.

Ex.

Qué mierda.   Not cool.

Esta mierda.   This shit.

Eres una mierda.   You are shit. / You are an asshole.

Chido

Chido is the main Mexislang way to say cool. Other ways to say cool are: De pelos, de huevos, padre, chingón, fregón, mamalón and verga. All are informal, but verga is the heaviest one, you wouldn't use it in front of your girlfriend's mom.

Ex.

Que chido está este libro. This book is very cool.

Chale

Chale is a very simple word, and it's used to express disappointment, or disagreement about something someone just told you. It also can be used as a slang term to say you are sorry about something that happened to someone.

Ex.

¿Quieres ver la nueva película de Superman? Wanna see the new Superman movie?

-Chale, si a mí ni me gustan las películas de superhéroes. - No, I don't even like superhero movies.

¿Vamos por una cerveza? Wanna go for a beer?

-No puedo, estoy de viaje. -I can´t, Im not in the city.

-Chale, pues avísame cuando regreses para ir por una.	-I see –dissapoinment-. Tell me when you come back, so we can go out for one.
Atropellaron a mi perro.	My dog got run over by a car.
-Chale güey, lo siento.	– Bummer, dude. I'm sorry.

Huevo

Huevo is a common word that is used for one of the most common foods: eggs. Also, it's the equivalent of "balls" in Mexican slang. It means both male genitalia or the virtues of braveness or boldness.

The expression ¡A huevo! is used to express a lot of satisfaction or accomplishment about something. It can also mean "of course", when someone asks you a question.

The expression De a huevo (not to be confused with A huevo), means someone is being forced to do something when they really don't want to.

Ex:

Solo se la pasa rascándose los huevos todo el día.	He spent his time scratching his balls all day. **(Being lazy)**
¡Tienes muchos huevos!	You have balls! **(Being brave)**
¡¡A huevo!! (When someone	Hell yeah!!

scores a touchdown)

| *De a huevo tengo que hacer el trabajo para pasar la materia.* | I really must do the project to pass the class. |

Culo

Culo is the slang way to say butt, but it also can be used to say someone is very mean or uncooperative. The word *ojete* (butthole), can also be used for this meaning.

You can also use a variation of *culo*, which is "*Culero*", but you can also use this other one to say something isn't good, or that you dislike it.

Ex.

Cuando era niño y le hacía bromas a mi hermano, mi madre me pegaba en el culo.	When I was a child, and I played pranks on my brother, my mom used to spank me.
No comas en ese restaurant, la comida está culera.	Don't eat at that restaurant. The food sucks.
Ese güey golpea perros, es bien culo/culero.	That dude hits dogs, he is an asshole.

Pendejo

Pendejo means a "single pubic hair", but it's almost never used with this meaning.

It has two main slang meanings, the first one is "dumbass". However, *pendejo* is quite a harsh word, even more than dumbass, so if you want to insult someone for his lack of intelligence without going too far, you can stick with *estúpido*, *tonto* or *menso*; which mean the same thing but in a softer way.

The second meaning of *pendejo* is asshole or jerk.

Ex:

No voy a regresar con mi exnovia, no soy pendejo.

I'm not getting back with my ex-girlfriend. I'm not a dumbass.

Ese pendejo no hizo nada en el equipo, y se llevó todos los elogios del jefe.

That asshole did nothing in the team, and got all the praise from the boss.

Chapter 2
Internet Slang

Character archetypes.

Mexican Spanish has changed a lot over the years, especially since the introduction of social media and the internet.

Thanks to it, now it's way easier for everybody to access new idioms and language trends, and a lot of character archetypes have been formed out of this, as well as a new vocabulary specific for each one.

The following are some of the most known and popular Mexislang character archetypes and stereotypes:

Mirrey

A *Mirrey* (Myking- with no space between the words) is commonly a young Mexican man, who is a member of the upper class, or tries to look like one. He always brags about the tons of money he or his family makes, however, his family might not even be that rich. He's always talking about his crazy adventures and wild lifestyle. Their dress code is always to have a shirt, two or three buttons undone, no matter if the weather is cold. Their lifestyle is based on glamour, prestige, consumerism, excess (or a disproportionate aspiration towards it), and elitism. They are a group of people who are always trying to be perceived as of higher value compared to the rest of the population in both real life, or social media regardless of whether they possess that higher social status at all. If you want to find a real example, google Roberto Palazuelos, or the singer Luis Miguel, who is even called Luis Mirrey by some people. The video-parodies *"Quiero ir al Antro"* and *"Acapulco Dreamers"* are also good and funny examples of what a *mirrey* is.

Lobuki

Mexican term used to describe upper class uptight girls. They are known for being in the company of one or more *mirreyes*, as they are a very important part of the *mirrey* lifestyle.

The pictures the *mirreyes* take with the *lobukis* serve as social proof that they are popular even with the most uptight girls, as *lobukis* rarely or almost never talk to someone who isn't a *mirrey*, because part of being a *lobuki* is to take advantage of the *mirreyes*, by getting gifts, alcohol and free rides in expensive cars.

Most *lobukis* aren't exclusive to a single *mirrey*, as they tend to go out with whoever offers them better things at the moment, but this doesn't mean they are easy girls, as many of them dump the guys after they aren't useful for them anymore.

The word *lobuki*, comes from *loba* (female wolf). Some *mirreyes* tend to finish their words with -uki like calling a nightclub (*antro*) *antruki*, or a party (*fiesta*) *fiestuki*.

Luchona

In Mexican slang, a *luchona (*fighter*)*, or *Mamá luchona*, is a young irresponsible single mother who still lives with her parents. This term became an internet meme, when some women posted on social networks that they were fighters and strong for raising their child all alone. It became a form of mockery, because lots of "*mamas luchonas*" live with their parents, go out to party and leave their kids with their grandparents, and are not mentally mature, resourceful, independent or responsible at all.

Bendición

Bendición actually means "blessing". However, in Mexislang, it refers to the offspring of the *luchona* mothers. The reason why we call them like that is because people here say that "A child is always a blessing" whenever an unplanned child is coming. People popularized the term "*bendición*" in social media and it's now used in modern Mexican slang with this meaning.

Mañoso/Narco

In Mexican slang, being called *mañoso*, or *de la maña,* means you have ties with Mexican organized crime. The term *narco* means that someone is a member of a drug cartel (It doesn't mean that someone is a member of the Drug Enforcement Police Department, quite the opposite). *Narco* has now become the Mexican equivalent of "gangster".

Buchón

In regular Spanish, a *buchón* is a dove that inhales a lot of air, making its body bigger to scare other males and attract females, but in Mexican slang, *buchón* can be used to refer to farmers that are related to the drug business in the state of Sinaloa, or to those who act and feel they are drug dealers themselves, when they aren't at all.

Similarly, the *buchones* you'll see in the cities are almost always overweight, and will try to make you think they are very wealthy, drink a lot of alcohol, and are the coolest guys ever while trying to look and act like a mix between a cowboy, a farmer, and a *narco*.

Their biggest heroes are Mexican gangsters and drug dealers, but they also relate to crime cinema characters like Tony Montana or Michael Corleone.

They tend to go to bars, and like to drink the cheapest Buchanan's bottle of whisky, thinking it's high class and very expensive even if it's only 30 dollars' worth at max. Some people even think the term *Buchones* comes from the name of this brand. They like to take and upload pictures with them with these bottles because music videos of *narcocorridos* (drug related folk songs) feature heavy product placement of this particular brand. Whenever possible, they appear with firearms on their pictures to look more tough.

They usually hear a lot of "banda" and "narcocorridos" songs. These are songs with lyrics about narco tales and stories. If you want to see examples of this Mexican subculture, you can search for "narcocorridos" on YouTube, or look up songs like "*camaro y hummer*", "*el patrón*", "*el niño sicario*", or "*trocas marcadas*".

Their dress code is similar to a *mirrey*, with lots of them having unbuttoned shirts, but they like to use fake leather boots, belts, hats and cheap imitations of expensive brand clothing to look more upper class. They also tend to act like there's no law above them and are untouchable.

If you want an example of a real *buchón*, search for "*El komander*", a singer of narcocorridos, or "el Ezequiel" a comedian that parodies *buchones*. As I said, most of them think, and act as if they were part of the Mexican mafia, but only a few of them really are, and you can tell from the expensive stuff they actually have.

BUCHÓN LANGUAGE.

Buchones have their own slang that has been popularized by the narcocorridos they sing, and TV dramas about narcos. Here you'll find some of their most used words:

Fierro: To go and execute someone with a gun. This is because *fierro* actually means iron, and guns (at least some of them) are made out of iron. So, when someone says "vamos a darle Fierro" means, "we are going to beat him down or kill him". It can also mean "Let's do it!", "We're on it!" or "Let's party!", especially when said in conjunction with *pariente*: *"Fierro pariente"*.

Pariente: "Blood related" in regular Spanish, but in *buchón* language it's used to refer to a friend. It's very similar to "bro" in American English.

Arre: It means let's go. Arre is the command people use in farms to make their horses start walking or running. So, it's the same with people.

Viejón: Dude or Friend. Usually used when you are going to make a suggestion or ask for a favor.

Encobijado (Covered in sheets): When someone is killed by the mafia, they usually cover the corpses of their victims in sheets which are called *cobijas* in Spanish. So, *encobijado*, means that someone was killed by the mafia.

Levantón: It means to kidnap. When a truck filled with *narcos* stops you when you are on your way to some place and they kidnap you, it's called a *levantón*. *Levantar* means "to lift", so it comes from lifting the victims from the streets into their vehicles.

Halcón: It literally means a falcon. Halcón is an informer or scout that works for the mafia, who is paid to be at a certain place to keep an eye on it while delivering info on what is happening to their superiors. Another word for the same thing is "maruchero"

Niño rata

Literally "ratboy", this is the name people in Mexico and Latin America have given to pre-adolescents with a squeaky voice, that spend most of their free time playing videogames online (most of them not intended for their age), and scream, yell and insult other players.

They tend to be very young, from, let's say, 8 to 15 years of age, and their biggest stars are YouTube videogame streamers, who they love almost religiously.

It became a very popular trend/internet meme.

If you do something mean to a player when you are playing online, you may get called "niño rata" in a teasing manner.

The real inspiration for this term is an early episode of the Simpsons, where Homer calls Bart a "Ratboy".

LANGUAGE OF RAT KIDS (Modern geeky internet slang)

As I already said before, rat kids are annoying young kids or teens on the internet. If you see or read their comments on Facebook or Youtube, you may not understand a lot of what they're saying. That's because Rat Kids have already developed a slang of their own, and a lot of it is even used by young adults on the internet now. Here are some of the most important words and expressions of modern internet slang in México and Latin América.

Arenoso: This literraly means sandy. Someone arenoso is someone who gets offended easily when someone criticizes them or something they like.

Ap: Stands for *amor platónico*, which means platonic love. They also use the English word *crush* with the same meaning.

Elfa: Spanish for a female elf, that's the usual *niño rata* way to say girl, or girlfriend.

Lince: Spanish for linx. It's the usual way a *niño rata* says boy.

Me encorazona: To send a heart emoji on a Facebook post. It literally means "it hearts me"

Me emputa / me emperra: To send and angry face emoji on a Facebook post. It literally means "it angries me"

Me enflorece: To send a thankful emoji on a Facebook publication. It literally means "it flowers me"

Me enjotece / me enjota / me enmaricona: To send a gay pride emoji on a Facebook post. It literally means "it gays me". This comes from the words *joto* and *maricón*. Both are very derogatory ways to call a homosexual man, the equivalent of *faggot*.

However, when the gay pride flag emoji was released, everybody, even homosexual people were using this expression to refer to this emoji, so it doesn't seem to be as homophobic as calling someone a *joto* or *maricón*.

Laura sad: It's a deformation of "la hora sad" which means "the sad hour". People use it when sharing sad memes and tales.

El Zelda: An internet link (because of Link, the main character of Nintendo's the Legend of Zelda series).

La dvd: The spelling of the word dvd in Spanish sounds a lot like "de verdad ", so people on the internet sometimes use this to say "the truth", or "truthfully". People also use "la Netflix" "la vhs" "la blu ray" "la Betamax" "la cd" to say la verdad in Latin American internet slang.

Repollo /repoio /rechicken: This means cabagge, and because the word sounds very similar to "repost", it means a publication was already published in that internet community in the past.

Chidori/shidori: As already explained, chido means cool, and chidori was a technique used in the manga/anime Naruto, which name sounds very similar so people on the internet started using it instead of chido, and it stuck.

Virgo: A virgin.

Ward: When someone likes a thread, that person writes "ward" on the post. They do this to keep track of the evolution of the thread, because they'll get new messages on their feedback after writing on it. This comes from the gaming term "guard" used in games of the MOBA genre, like League of Legends and Dota2.

Pack: It comes from the English word "pack", and it's used to talk about a pack of pictures of a woman, that may or may not be sexual in content. "Pasa el pack" (share your pack) is like the Latin American way to say "send me some nudes".

Papu/Perro/Perrazo: Dude.

Nepe: Masculine sexual organ.

Momo: Meme

Momazo: Very good meme.

Naik: Like.

Gfa: From *jefa*, which means *mother* in Mexican slang

Chairo

Radical Far-Left supporters in Mexican politics are called *Chairos*. They are against globalization and capitalism, they think the US is the most evil country in the world and they will insult you if you disagree with them.

They will always talk trash about the PRI and the PAN (Mexican right-wing political parties) and will always support MORENA, Mexico's main far-left political party.

Their biggest hero is Andres Manuel Lopez Obrador (also known as AMLO or "El Peje"). The current president of Mexico.

People also may call radical Far-Right supporters, "Derechairos", but chairos was the original slang from wich that one came from.

Únicas y diferentes

As you may have noticed, Mexicans make fun of everything and everyone. In Facebook and other social media, a group of girls started posting stuff saying that they didn't like to party, they didn't care about beauty, they preferred to drink coffee, read books and watch good movies. These girls were nicknamed "Únicas y Diferentes", which means "Unique and Different".

A "única y diferente" is a girl, who always claims that she's not like the regular girls, she doesn't care about beauty, make up, or other feminine things and she's into the current trends, like the hottest young adult novel at the moment, or the most popular superhero movies.

Some people also call them "únicas y detergentes". This archetype is the Mexican equivalent of special snowflake, and it's used also for men, but mostly to make fun of them when they brag about how their niche tastes in music, movies or hobbies are better than the ones most people have.

Nini

It comes from the phrase "ni estudias, ni trabajas" (You don't even study and you don't even work), and it means exactly that. A Nini is a young person who doesn't have an occupation nor goes to school, and just hangs around with his friends while living with his or her parents.

Juniors

Very similar to *Ninis*, *Juniors* are spoiled upper class sons or daughters that have a lot of stuff given to them by their families. They may study or work, but all their stuff is inherited, and they got it without making any real effort. They may or not be braggy about it. Some juniors are actually very nice people, and not stuck up at all, but they are still juniors, because they have lots of things that they got without working for them.

Ladys and lords

A person that did something very extreme or over the top in a video that went viral. For example, once, a young drunk girl had a car accident, and when the authorities were arresting her, she tried to bribe them with 100 pesos (5 to 7 dollars). She went viral, and everyone was calling her lady 100 pesos.

Cholo

A *cholo*, or *chola*, is a person whose outfit is a Mexicanized version of the hip hop fashion style. *Cholos* are usually teenagers from street gangs, and tend to wear forehead bandanas, short pants, shirts twice their size, black lipstick if they are girls, and black inked tattoos with religious motifs.

Their looks and trends always change with time. Not all people that dress like *cholos* have bad intentions, but still, you must be careful, because *cholos* are usually street thugs, or members of gangs made up of young, lower class people from urban areas in Mexico, like the street market of Tepito, in Mexico City.

Don vergas

The equivalent of "Mr. Almighty" in Mexican slang. A don vergas is someone who doesn't give a damn about rules in general, like traffic lights, getting in the back of a line, or respecting the parking lot for disabled people. A don vergas breaks all sorts of social rules or traffic norms and gets angry when someone complains about it or whenever they get arrested by the police.

Godínez

This term is mostly used when talking about office workers, but it can also be used for working class people, with an averge or low salary.

While there are many theories about the origin of this word, the most accepted one is the character "Godínez" from the Mexican comedy show "El chavo". This character was a kid who always tried doing the least possible amount of work he could, and never wanted to stand out in the classroom, so that he wouldn't have any extra responsabilities, as many office workers do here in Mexico.

Fifí

This is an old word that became a trend after the actual president (AMLO) used it during his speeches. In real Spanish it´s used as a way to call someone who shows off a lot, and is always following trends, but in modern Mexican slang it´s used for mainly two things, as a despective way to call Mexican high class people, or as a derrogative way to call someone who opposes and contradicts the current president and his left party.

Chapter 3
MexiSayings and Expressions

Across many generations, Mexicans have created tons of expressions to refer to many different situations and life lessons. This chapter is one of the longest in the book as it contains a recompilation of proverbs and expressions commonly used in the country, and while a lot of them may get lost in translation, because of wordplay or language specific double entendre, the examples and explanations given here will make it easier to grasp the real meaning of these Mexican words of wisdom.

Taparle el ojo al macho

Literally it means *"to cover the eye of a male"*, and it's a sentence used to say you are going to cover something you did (may or not be something shady or illegal), so no one notices.

Ex.

Le tapamos el ojo al macho a nuestros gastos, para no pagar impuestos.

We covered our expenses, to evade paying taxes.

Hacerse pato

Literally "to turn oneself into a duck". Its real meaning is "to play dumb".

Ex.

Mi exnovio está celoso de ti, pero se está haciendo pato hablando con mi hermano.

My ex-boyfriend is jealous of you, but he is playing dumb talking to my brother.

Sacar la sopa

Literally "to take the soup out". This expression means that you are making someone tell you the truth about something or simply, getting out information from them that they consider to be secret or may be reluctant to tell you.

Ex.

Voy a sacarle la sopa sobre cómo consiguió su fortuna.

I'm going to make him tell me how he got his fortune.

¿Nos peinamos o nos hacemos trenzas?

"Do we comb our hair, or do we make pigtails?" It's an expression used to ask which of 2 or more options will a group of people pick.

Ex.

Podemos ir a la playa, o al cine, entonces, ¿nos peinamos, o nos hacemos trenzas?

We can go to the beach or to the movies. So, which one is it going to be?

En menos de lo que canta un gallo

This sentence literally means "sooner than a rooster can sing" And it means very fast.

Ex.

Llegaste en menos de lo que canta un gallo. — You came here very fast.

En corto

It literally means "shortly", and it's an expression used to say that you'll do something fast, or to make someone hurry up. You can also say "en cortinas", "de volada" or "de volón". Another slang expression for very fast is "de volón pinpón".

Another use for "en corto" is to say that a place, or a person, is very near.

Ex.

¡En corto! sino ya no funcionará. — Hurry up! or it won't work.

Mi casa queda en corto de aquí. — My house is near here.

Llegaré de volada. — I'll arrive soon.

Ser un estuche de monerías

It literally means "*To be a suitcase full of cute items*", and this expression is used to refer to someone who has a lot of skills, that make him, or her interesting or attractive.

Ex.

-*Sabe cocinar, bailar, cantar, tocar guitarra y preparar cerveza artesanal.*

– ¡Vaya!, es un estuche de monerías.

-He can cook, dance, sing, play guitar, and make craft beer.

– Wow, he has a ton of interesting skills.

Atáscate que hay lodo

Literally *"Get full of it, because there's mud"*. It's used to express that you have a lot of something, or you have temporary freedom to do whatever you want, so you must enjoy the chance and get all you can. It's very similar to the American expression *"knock yourself out"*.

Ex.

Me regalaron tres sacos de mango, así que ahora, atásquense, que hay lodo.

They gave me three sacks of mango. So now, eat all you can while it lasts.

Por si las moscas

This literally translates to "just in case flies appear", and it's used as an equivalent of "just in case".

Ex.

No sé si mi perrito regresará a casa, pero dejaré la puerta abierta en la noche por si las moscas.

I don't know if my doggie is coming back home, but I'll let the door open tonight, just in case.

Ser ajonjolí de todos los moles

It literally means "to be sesame of every mole". Mole is a Mexican dish that uses many ingredients and has many different versions, but most of them use sesame in one way or another. Since you can find sesame in almost any version of mole, being called an "*ajonjolí de todos lo moles*" means that you are always present at every party or important event, or that you are a member of a lot of different social clubs. It can also be used to say a man, or a woman has had a lot of romantic/sexual partners.

Ex.

Ella es muy sociable. Es ajonjolí de todos los moles.

She is very social. She is at every party.

Hacer changuitos

"To make little monkeys". The meaning of this expression is "to cross your fingers" as a lucky charm.

Ex.

Mandé una solicitud para entrar a la Universidad, haz changuitos para que me acepten.

I sent an application for college. Cross your fingers so they accept me.

Echarle mucha crema a tus tacos

"To put a lot of cream on your tacos". It's used to express someone braqgs a lot, and thinks a lot of himself or herself, even if he or she may or may not live up to that.

Ex.

Es buen jugador, pero a nadie le agrada, porque le echa mucha crema a sus tacos.

He is a good player, but nobody likes him because he brags way too much.

Planchar oreja

This expression means that someone is sleeping. It literally means "to iron an ear", and this is because, when you sleep sideways, your ear gets flat because it's under the weight of your whole head, like the wrinkles on the clothes get flat when you iron them.

Ex.

No molestes a tu hermano. Trabajó toda la noche y está planchando oreja.	Don't bother your brother. He worked all night, and now he is sleeping.

Oir pasos en la azotea

It literally means "to hear steps on the rooftop", and it's used to express when someone is feeling paranoid, or when someone is overthinking their problems, or feeling unsafe about stuff they don't have control over, like overpopulation, climate change, etc.

Ex.

No sé si mi novia me engaña o solo estoy oyendo pasos en la azotea.	I don't know if my girlfriend is cheating on me, or I'm just being paranoid about it.

El que es perico donde quiera es verde

Literally it means "A parrot is green everywhere", and it's used to express that if you are good at something, you are good at it no matter the place or situation.

Ex.

No tengo miedo de no encontrar trabajo en un país donde no hablen mi idioma. El que es perico, donde quiera es verde.	I'm not afraid of not finding a job in a country where my native language is not spoken. If you are good at something, you're good at it no matter what.

Vamos a ver de qué lado masca la iguana

Literally it means, *"let's see from which side the iguana chews"*, and it real means "let's see who is the best between you and me" (or between two people or things).

Ex.

Por fin esos boxeadores van a pelear, ahora sí vamos a ver de qué lado masca la iguana.	Finally, those boxers are going to fight. Now we'll finally see who is the best.

Estar como agua para chocolate

In some places in rural México, people use boiling water instead of milk to make chocolate. This expression, literally means, "to be like hot water for chocolate".

Because of this, the meaning of this expression is to have very intense feelings, but it's used mostly to talk about anger, or sexual arousal.

Ex.

Estoy como agua para chocolate. I'm mad/ I'm aroused.

Es puro pájaro nalgón

This expression literally means "He's a bird with a big butt", We use it to refer to someone who is always telling lies or exaggerates everything. It's the equivalent of *"bullshitter"* or *"full of shit"*.

Ex.

No creas las promesas de ese hombre. Es puro pájaro nalgón. Don't believe that man's promises. He's full of shit.

Me cae / Me cae bien / Me cae mal

Me cae, literally means "something falls into me", but in Mexican slang, it's used to say you are sure about something. Also, to add more emphasis on how sure someone is, people often use the phrase: Me cae de a madre.

Me cae bien or Me cae mal have completely different meanings. We use these expressions to say that we like or dislike someone or also, whether something we ate made us sick or not.

Ex.

- ¿Te cae que va a llover mañana?	- Are you sure tomorrow will rain?
-Me cae.	-I'm sure of it.
-Esa chava es buena onda, me cae bien.	-That chick is cool, I like her.
-No debí comer burritos, siempre me caen mal.	I shouldn't have eaten burritos, they always make me sick.

Brincos dieras

This expression literally means "You would be jumping", and it's really used as a Mexican slang equivalent of "you wish".

Ex.

-Voy a ganar la lotería.	-I'm going to win the lottery.
-Brincos dieras.	– Yeah, you wish.

Echarse su taco

Darse, or echarse su taco, is a sentence that literally means "to give yourself your own taco", and has the same meaning as "To treat oneself", but it's also used when someone thinks too highly of himself, or when someone rejects something because they think they deserve better.

Ex.

Me voy a dar mi taco y comprarme un carro nuevo.	I'm going to treat myself with a new car.
Esa chica rechaza a todos los hombres del pueblo. Se está dando su taco.	That girl rejects all men in town. She thinks no one deserves her.

El horno no está para los bollos

This expression literally means "The oven is not ready yet to make the bread", and it simply means that something, or someone isn't ready.

Ex.

-¿Te dieron el préstamo?	-Did they give you the loan?
-El horno no está para los bollos.	-It's not ready yet.

Por detroit

Mexican slang expression used to say, "*from behind*". This is because Detroit sounds very similar to the Spanish word "*detrás*" which means behind.

Ex.

-¿Cómo entraste, si la puerta principal estaba cerrada?

-Por detroit.

-How did you get in, if the front door was closed.

- I used the backdoor.

Estar cura

It means that something is funny. People also use the expression: *estar botana*, for the same meaning. Botana means "snacks" in English.

Ex.

Está bien botana tu disfraz de Halloween.

Your Halloween costume is very funny.

Esa película está super cura.

That movie is super funny.

De chocolate

In regular Spanish, this means "made out of chocolate", but in Mexican slang, it means something isn't serious or real.

Ex.

Vamos a jugar póker, pero las apuestas son de chocolate.

We'll play poker, but we won't be playing for real.

Son novios, pero de chocolate. Solo tienen 5 años.

They are boyfriend and girlfriend, but not for real. They are only 5 years old.

Dar atole con el dedo

Atole, is a Mexican drink made of cornstarch, with many different ingredients, flavors and recipes.

Literally "*Dar atole con el dedo*" means that someone is offering you a taste of their Atole and instead of using a spoon to give you a sip, that person uses his finger. Of course, the atole is going to fall down from his finger and you will end up tasting almost nothing.

What it figuratively means is "to be played as a fool", "to be conned" or to be "outsmarted by someone". It's the equivalent of "to be played like a violin".

Ex.

Hizo como que estaba enamorada de ti, pero al final te dio atole con el dedo.

She made you believe that she was in love with you, but she just played you like a violin.

Me late

Me late, comes from "latir", which means beat, like heartbeat. In Mexican slang it's used to say you like or approve of something.

Ex.

Me late tu carro.	I like your car.
Me late tu plan.	I agree with your plan.

Ser cuchillito de palo

It means, "to be a little wooden knife", and in Mexican slang it's used to express someone is annoying by being very insistent on something, it can be a request, or just an affirmation about something.

Ex.

Ya te dije que sí te lo voy a comprar, no estés como cuchillito de palo.	I told you already I'm going to buy it. Stop asking me so often about it.

Bajar avión

When you are under the influence of alcohol, or drugs, and you eat something or ingest any other substance to diminish your hangover. It literally means to "get out of the plane".

Ex.

Me siento un poco pedo. Vamos a comer unos tacos para bajar avión.

I feel a little drunk. Let's go eat some tacos to get out of this hangover.

Dar el avión

It literally means, "giving someone the airplane". In Mexican slang it means agreeing with someone only so that they can stop bothering you.

Ex.

Era muy molesto, le dije que nos veríamos otra vez, pero solo le di el avión.

He was very annoying. I told him we'll see each other again, but I just said that to get him out of my neck.

Ser concha

It literally means to be a seashell. In Mexican slang, if you are a seashell it means that you are a freeloader. A parasite to your friends, family and society.

By the way, *concha*, alone, without the verb to be, means female genitalia in Mexislang.

Ex.

Yo pago las cervezas hoy. Tu pagaste la vez pasada, no hay

I'll pay for the beers today. You paid for them last time, I don't want to be a freeloader.

que ser concha.

¿Y tu nieve de que la quieres?

It could be translated as "…and which flavor of ice cream should I bring you?" and it's used to express in a sardonic manner that you won't do something you are being told to, or that someone expects you to do, or to be. It's like saying "sure, and what else?" in a very sarcastic way.

Ex.

-De ahora en adelante somos novios.	From now on, we are in a relationship.
-¿Novios? ¿Y tu nieve de qué la quieres?	In a relationship? Sure, anything else?

Sin chiste

It literally means without a joke. What this expression really means is that something is very ordinary, too simple and not special at all. It's a way of expressing that something or someone is unremarkable.

Ex.

Este trabajo no tiene chiste.   This job is not (challenging /fun /exciting) at all.

Ella tiene un novio muy guapo,   She has a very handsome

pero sin chiste.   boyfriend, but he is pretty boring.

Echar la firma

It literally means, "to write a signature". This is what you say, between men, to express that you are going to leave to urinate. It's the Mexican slang equivalent of "I'm gonna go to take a leak".

Ex.

Miguel debe estar enfermo de su riñón, va muy seguido a echar la firma.

Miguel must have something wrong with his kidney. He goes to take a leak way too often.

¿A qué hora sales por el pan?

It literally means "at what time do you go out to buy some bread?". It's a common phrase men use to flirt with women. It implies that he is so attracted to her, that he will be there at the bakery at the time she comes, only to see her or hangout with her for a little while.

It's just a clever way to express that you find someone attractive.

Ex.

Oye, ¿y tu hermana a qué hora sale por el pan?

Hey, your sister is a real knockout.

De a grapa

In Spanish, *grapa* means staple. But in Mexican slang, people use this expression to say something is free, as in you don't have to pay for it. This is because "free" in Spanish is *gratis* which sounds like *grapa*.

Ex.

| *Gané un premio dentro de este dulce, y me dieron otro de a grapa.* | I won a prize inside this candy bar, and they gave me another one for free. |

Alborotar el gallinero

This is an expression people use when someone very attractive makes people around him or her go crazy with infatuation. It literally means "to disturb or excite the hen house".

Ex.

| *Si vas vestida así a la fiesta, vas a alborotar el gallinero.* | If you're going to the party dressed like that, all the guys are going to be throwing themselves at you. |

Aquí nada más mis chicharrones truenan

It literally means "Here, my pork rinds are the only ones that crack". The real meaning of the expression is, "Here I'm the one who takes all the decisions". It's a Mexican equivalent of "My way or the highway".

Ex.

Soy el jefe de esta compañía. Aquí nada más mis chicharrones truenan.	I'm the boss of this company. Here, I'm the one who calls all the shots.

A caballo regalado no se le ve el diente

It literally means "you don't check the teeth of a horse that was given to you as a gift". It's used to express that when someone gives you a present, you shouldn't be criticizing it.

Me regalaron una consola de videojuegos sin controles, pero a caballo regalado no se le mira el diente.	They gave me a videogame console as a gift. It doesn't have any controllers, but it doesn't matter. After all, it was a gift.

Está cañón

It literally means "It's a cannon". We use it to express that something is hard, tough or complicated. People also tend to say "*está cabrón*" or "*está perro*" to express the same thing.

Ex.

Escribir un libro está cañón.   Writing a book is a tough deal.

No dar paso sin huarache

A *huarache* is a shoe, like a sandal, but made by indigenous people, with materials taken from nature, like palm tree, corn leaf, and/or different animal skin. This sentence literally means, "you don't give a step without a huarache" and means, you never do anything, without being 100% sure of it.

Ex.

No estoy seguro si me conviene ese negocio, no voy a dar paso sin huarache.   I'm not sure this business is convenient for me, I won't go ahead with it unless I'm 100% sure.

Ya salió el peine

It literally means "the comb just came out", but you use it to express the truth came to light about something.

Ex.

Ya salió el peine sobre quién se comió mi pastel de chocolate.   Now, I know the truth about who ate my chocolate cake.

Traer el Jesús en la boca

This expression literally means "having Jesus in my mouth" and it's the Mexislang way to express being concerned or worried about something.

Ex.

Es muy tarde y mi esposo no ha llegado a casa. Ando con el Jesús en la boca.	It's late and my husband hasn't arrived home. I'm dead worried.

Me hace lo que el viento a Juárez

This expression is referring to Benito Juarez, one of the most important presidents in Mexico's history and it literally means "It does to me what the wind did to Juárez". It's real meaning is "It doesn't bother/affect me".

There are certain myths about the origin of this expression. One of the most popular ones relates to a painting of the president holding a Mexican flag. In the painting, the flag is drawn with a lot of wind waves, like if the president and the flag were facing an intense wind current. However, unlike the flag, the appearance of the president looks impeccable. His suit and his hair appear to be completely unaffected by the wind. The president seems to be immune to everything that's going on.

Ex.

Yo no me emborracho fácil, el alcohol me hace lo que el viento a Juárez.

I don't get drunk easily. Alcohol doesn't affect me.

Dar el gatazo

This expression means that something is good enough.

Ya vente vestido así. Sí das el gatazo.

Come dressed like that. You look good enough.

Dar el rol

To go for a walk or to explore some new location.

Ex.

No quiero quedarme en el hotel. Quiero salir a dar el rol.

I don't want to stay at the hotel room. I want to go out and see things.

Pasarse de tueste

This expression literally means "to roast something more than you should have". It is used to express that a person has gone too far with something, but it's less harsh than other similar expressions like *pasarse de verga, de corneta, de camote,* and *de lanza.* It's still a very informal expression.

Ex.

Te pasaste de tueste poniéndole chicle en el cabello. You went too far putting bubblegum in her hair.

Hacer un pancho

To make a huge deal or to exaggerate something that is not too important.

Ex.

Si no contesto rápido sus mensajes, mi novia me hace un pancho. If I don't answer her messages quickly, my girlfriend makes a huge drama about it.

No pega ni con chicle

This phrase literally means "It doesn't even stick with bubblegum". You say this when something is hopeless, and you have tried everything, but you just can't accomplish a task or make something work out.

Ex.

Intentamos ser solo amigos, pero eso no pegó ni con chicle. We tried to be friends, but that just didn't work out.

Colgar los tenis

It literally means: "to hang up your tennis shoes". You use this phrase to express that someone died. It is the Mexican equivalent of "to kick the bucket".

Ex.

Él estaba muy enfermo y no se movía. Parece que colgó los tenis.

He was very sick, and he didn't move. I think he kicked the bucket.

Di rana y yo salto

It translates to "Say frog, and I'll jump". It means: "For me to do it, you just need to say it".

Ex.

-¿Nos subimos a la montaña rusa?

-Di rana, y yo salto.

-Do we ride the rollercoaster?

-You just have to say it.

Ya rugiste

This phrase literally means, "you already roared" and it's used as the Mexican equivalent of "you said it" when you agree to do something with someone.

Sometimes people add "*león*" at the end of the sentence, just to make it sound cooler.

People sometimes say the expression *"ya dijiste"* which has the same meaning.

Ex.

-*Tengo hambre, vamos por tacos.*

-I'm hungry. Let's go get some tacos.

-*Ya rugiste.*

-You said it.

Agarrar de su puerquito

This phrase literally means: "To take someone as a little pig". When people bully you, take advantage of your good will or make a lot of mean jokes about you, you have become their "little pig". This is because in farms, little pet pigs are quite mistreated, abused and disrespected.

It's the Mexican equivalent of "becoming someone's bitch".

Ex.

Tienes que ser más rudo, si no te van a agarrar de su puerquito.

You need to be more tough, else they're going to make you their bitch.

Hablando del rey de Roma

"Speaking about the King of Rome", it is actually the Spanish equivalent of "Speak of the devil".

Ex.

A Manuel le gusta mucho esta canción. Hablando del rey de Roma, mira quién está aquí.	Manuel really likes this song. Speak of the devil. Look who's here.

Mal del Puerco

It could be translated as: "The pork's malaise" and it refers to the feeling of drowsiness we experience after eating a big meal, and we just want to take a nap and avoid working.

Ex.

Si comes mucho te va a dar el mal del puerco.	If you eat that much, you'll get all sleepy and tired.

Ya te cargó el payaso

Literally: "The clown has taken you away". It means that something terrible has happened to you or it's about to happen to you.

Many people believe that the origin of this expression comes from the universal fear of clowns that most people experience, however, it appears that this expression actually originated in the world of Rodeo Riding. In a Rodeo competition, when a cowboy is riding a mad bull or horse, there's always two (or more) people inside the field, paying close attention to what's happening and intervening whenever the rider falls. These assistants are called "*payasos*" which means clowns in Spanish. Their job is to distract the animal in whatever way possible so that it doesn't attack the rider and if the rider gets badly injured, it's their duty to take him out of the field as fast as possible. So, if you are a rider and you got carried out of the field by a clown, it means that you have failed and you got badly injured.

Ex.

La maestra te sorprendió copiando en el examen. Ya te cargó el payaso.	The teacher caught you cheating on the exam. You are in big trouble.

Barajéamela más despacio

It's a way of requesting someone to explain you something in a slower and clearer way. Its literal translation is: "Shuffle the card deck more slowly".

Ex.

-Necesitas usar el ICT para poder acceder al TPA y así vas logar generar PTPs para tu GCE.	-You need to use the ICT in order to access the TPA. That way, you will be able to generate PTPs for your GCE.
	-Ok, ok. Could you give me a

-A ver, a ver. Barajéamela más despacio. better and slower explanation?

No cantas mal las rancheras

In Mexican slang this means that "you aren't that bad" or you are actually "quite competent" at something. Its literal translation is: "You don't sing country songs that bad".

Ex.

María juega muy bien baloncesto, pero Azucena no canta mal las rancheras. María is very good at basketball, but Azucena isn't bad at all either.

Andar pariendo cuates

In slang, this expression means that you are in deep pain, you are in serious trouble or you are about to perform a very difficult task. Its literal meaning is: "to deliver twins", because it compares the intense pain women experience while going through this with your situation.

Ex.

Estudia hoy o vas a andar pariendo cuates el día del examen. You should study today, or you'll be having a hard time the day of the evaluation.

Ir a mi arbolito

We use this expression to say that we are going to urinate. Its literal meaning is: "To go to my little tree". This expression is actually a word play because the word *"mi"* and the first syllable of the word for little tree *"ar"*, sound a lot like the word *"mear"* when they are said together. *"Mear"* means to take a leak in Spanish slang.

Ex.

Voy a mi arbolito. I'm going to take a leak.

Hacer del uno / Hacer del dos

"Hacer del uno" means peeing and *"Hacer del dos"* means pooping.

Ex.

No hemos parado en todo el viaje, y necesito hacer del dos. We haven't stopped during the whole trip, I need to take a dump.

Comerse la torta antes del recreo

In Mexican slang, this means a girl got pregnant way too young, before finishing school or becoming a proper adult. It literally means: "To eat your lunch before recess".

Ex.

Lilia ya no va a la escuela porque se comió la torta antes del recreo.	Lilia doesn't go to school anymore, because she got pregnant.

Dar una mochada

"*Mochar*" means "to cut something with a machete" and "*mochada*" literally means "A slice cut made with a machete". The expression "to give someone a machete slice" means that you are bribing someone. In a way, you are giving someone a slice of your money to bribe them.

Ex.

El tránsito me detuvo, pero le di una mochada y me dejó ir.	The police officer pulled me over, but I bribed him, and he let me go.

Because of this expression, the verb *mochar* has now evolved and it has acquired the meaning of: "to pay for something or to give money for something".

Ponerse la del puebla

It literally means "to put on the shirt of Puebla's soccer team" and it's an indirect reference to the verb "*mochar*" with its same slang meaning. The reason why people make a connection between this team's shirt and the verb "*mochar*" is because, if you look at the shirt of Puebla's soccer team you will see that it is white with a big blue diagonal stripe that covers the entire chest. This big blue diagonal stripe looks like a slice cut or a "*mochada*". So, if you are "putting on the shirt of Puebla's team" or you are asking someone to do so, it means that person will have to pay or give money for something.

Ex.

| *Si quieres pasar al antro, ponte la del puebla.* | If you want to get into the night club, you'll have to give me some money. |

Ponerse las pilas

In Mexican slang, *ponerse las pilas* (put batteries on yourself), means you are motivated to put all your attention, effort an energy into something, so you won't get taken by surprise, and to do the best work you can on that task. It's the Mexican slang equivalent of *"Turn on the juice"*.

Ex.

| *Todavía puedes pasar el semestre. Ponte las pilas.* | You still can save the semester. Turn on the juice. |

Caer gordo

"To fall fatly". In Mexican slang, if someone falls fatly on you, it means you dislike this person. And if you are the one who falls fatly on someone, it means this person doesn't like you.

Ex.

No iré a la fiesta porque me cae gordo tu novio.

I won't go to the party because I don't like your boyfriend

Estar salado

It literally means being salty, but in Mexican slang it means that you are "unlucky".

Ex.

He comprado billetes de lotería por años y nunca he ganado. Estoy bien salado.

I've bought lottery tickets for years and I've never won. I'm so unlucky.

Mame / El tren del mame

In modern Mexican slang, *el mame* can mean two things: Alcohol or modern trends.

When someone says something like *"me subí al tren del mame"* it means that person has started to follow a particular trend about a subject. It's another way of saying "To follow the crowd".

Ex.

No te vayas, aún queda mucho mame y la noche es joven.

Don't go. There's still a lot of alcohol left, and the night is young.

A todo el mundo le gusta esa canción, pero no quiero ser

Everybody likes that song, but I don't want to become a fanboy *parte de ese mame.* such as everyone.

Sacar canas verdes

Hairs that start to become white when you get older, are called, "*canas*" in Spanish.

Sacar canas verdes (to grow green hair), means that something is driving you mad to the point of altering your natural hair color.

Ex.

La cancioncita del camión de helados me está sacando canas verdes.   The jingle of the ice cream truck is making me go mad.

No tener pelos en la lengua

"Without any hairs in the mouth". In Mexican slang, this means that you are not afraid to say what you think or to state how you feel about something.

Ex.

Esa mujer es muy directa. No tiene pelos en la lengua.   That woman is very straightforward. She tells it like it is.

Pegarle al gordo

Literally it means, "hitting the fat man", but the real meaning of "Pegarle al gordo" in Mexican slang is winning the lottery, or a big prize in a contest. It can also mean to be lucky about something.

Ex.

| *Le pegaste al gordo con tu novia.* | You were so lucky to find that girlfriend of yours. |
| *Compré casi todos los boletos de lotería. Estoy seguro que voy a pegarle al gordo.* | I've bought almost all the lottery tickets. I'm sure I'm going to hit the jackpot. |

Al chile

It means something you said is the actual truth or you are giving a sincere opinion.

This is also a very informal phrase, used between close friends, and it's the equivalent of saying "To be honest" "I'm not kidding" or "I mean it".

Ex.

| *Al chile, no quiero ir a la cena familiar.* | To be honest, I don't want to go to the family dinner. |

Sana, sana, colita de rana

This is a very popular nursery rhyme that a mother usually sings when a child gets hurt and she is attending his wound. The entire rhyme goes like this:

"Sana, sana, colita de rana. Si no sana hoy, sanará mañana."

It could be translated as: "Heal, heal, little frog tail. Tomorrow it will heal if it doesn't heal today".

La venganza de Moctezuma

"Moctezuma's vengeance"

Moctezuma, was one of the last Aztec kings. He was the leader of the Aztec Empire at the time of the Spanish Invasion in Mexico which resulted in the demise of the Aztec civilization. Once the conquistadors had control over Tenochtitlan (ancient Mexico), they soon became fond of Aztec cuisine, eating all sorts of banquets. However, the Spaniards were not used to all the spicy ingredients in Mexican food. Therefore, a lot of them ended up getting sick, suffering from indigestion and diarrhea, some of them, even dying. This was known as "Moctezuma's vengeance", as if the Aztec Emperor was cursing them from the afterlife through Mexican cuisine.

Nowadays, when a foreigner comes to visit Mexico and gets sick because all the food that he ate here was just too much for his stomach, we call that *"La venganza de Moctezuma"*.

Ex.

Mi amigo de Alemania se comió como quince tacos. Le gustaron mucho, pero ayer en la noche le cayó la venganza de Moctezuma.

My friend from Germany ate like fifteen tacos. He liked them a lot, but last night, Moctezuma's vengeance fell upon him (he got sick).

Caerte el veinte

Caerte el veinte, is a phrase you say when you finally get the meaning of something, like a joke, or something from school, after having trouble understanding it at first. It's also used when a stubborn person finally stops doing something annoying or they finally start following orders.

Ex.

-Entonces, ¿solo tengo que elevar este número al cuadrado y luego multiplicarlo por este otro?

-Así es, ya te cayó el veinte.

-So, I only have to raise this number to the second power and then multiply it by this other one?

-Yes, now you got it.

Ya le dije que no quiero salir con él, pero todavía no le cae el veinte.

I already told him that I don't want to date him, but he still doesn't get it.

Te hace falta barrio

Literally, it means "you lack neighborhood". What it really means is that you lack street smarts.

Ex.

-No sé cómo tomar el metro en Ciudad de México.	-I don't know how to take the subway in Mexico City.
-Te hace falta barrio.	-You lack street smarts.

Tener el nopal en la cara

This phrase could be translated as "having a cactus on your face". It means someone looks really Mexican because of his or her looks (brown skin, dark hair and indigenous facial features).

Ex.

Nadie te va a creer que eres gringo. Tienes el nopal en la cara.	No one is going to believe you're American. You look Mexican all the way.

Buena onda/mala onda/ ¿qué onda?

Onda literally means wave, but in Mexican slang it can be used to describe one's personality or character.

If you are "a good wave" (*Buena onda*) it means that you're nice, likable or cool.

If you are "a bad wave" (*Mala onda*) it essentially means that you're an asshole.

There's also "*Qué mala onda*" which is the Mexican slang way of saying: "What a shame" or "what a tragedy" after hearing something bad happening to someone. And "*Qué buena onda*" which is like: "that's awesome" or "great for you" after hearing something good happening to someone.

Lastly, we have the famous slang greeting of "¿Qué onda?" which means "What's up?".

In all this expression, *onda* can be changed to *rollo* or *pedo* and still conserve the same meaning. *buena onda, buen rollo, buen pedo*, they all mean the same thing.

Example

-El nuevo profe de mate se ve que es bien estricto.	The new math teacher seems really strict.
-Para nada, lo tuve el año pasado. Es buena onda.	-Not at all, I know him from last year. He's cool.
Ese vato es mala onda. No me ayudó y yo siempre lo he ayudado.	That dude is an asshole. He didn't help me, and I have always helped him.
¡¿Qué onda, güey!?	What's up, dude?!

De tín, Marín

It comes from: "De tín, Marín, de do pingüé" which is the Mexican equivalent of: "Eeny, meeny, miny, moe". The expression *De tín, Marín* just means to choose something randomly.

Ex.

| *No sabía cuál elegir, así que agarré este de tín, marín.* | I didn't know which one to choose, so I ended up picking this one randomly. |

De pelos

It's another Mexican slang term to say that something is "cool". Literally, it means "hairy" or "made out of hairs". Other ways to say something is cool in Mexican slang are: *verga, chido, padre, chingón, fregón, perrón, mamalón*.

Ex.

| *Esta fiesta está de pelos.* | This party is so cool. |

Dar lata

Literally, to give a can. You use this term to say something is annoying, insisting, or troublesome. You can also use latoso, and latosa, as adjectives, to express the same.

Ex.

| *Dan mucha lata los vecinos con su música ruidosa.* | The neighbours are very anoying with their loud music. |

De panzaso

Panzaso, means hitting someone or something with the belly. But the expression "de panzaso", is used as the equivalent of "by the skin of your teeth."

Examples:

Aprobé el examen de panzaso.
I approved the test by the skin of my teeth.

Manita de gato

A quick fix or makeover you do to something or someone.

Examples:

No puedes salir luciendo así, dejame darte una manita de gato.
You can't go out looking like that, let me give you a quick makeover

Media naranja

Half orange. It's the mexislang equivalent of "Your other half" or "your soulmate"

Examples:

Encontre mi media naranja en linea.

I found my soulmate online.

La pinta

Mexican slang for when you go to another place instead of school and skip the whole day.

Examples:

Mañana vamos a hacernos la pinta e ir a mi casa a jugar videojuegos.

We'll skip clases the whole day tomorrow, and we'll go to my house to play videogames.

Chapter 4
Mexislang verbs

Expressing actions through slang verbs is one of the skills that people who are learning or studying Spanish in Mexico must master to sound more like a native. Being able to use these verbs, conjugate them correctly, making verbs into nouns, and vice versa, is essential to survive in a Mexican social environment. Here is a list of the most important verbs in mexislang, as well as their respective explanations and examples. It is important to note that all of these verbs are regular verbs when it comes to conjugation.

Pichicatear

To figure out how you can get what you need with limited budget.

Ex.

| *No tenemos mucho dinero, así que habrá que pichicatear para hacer esta fiesta.* | We don't have a lot of money, so we'll have to figure out how to have the party within our limited budget. |

Chiflar

To spoil someone. Literally, it means "to whistle".

Ex.

Le doy demasiados regalos a mi novia. La chiflo demasiado. | I give a lot of gifts to my girlfriend. I spoil her way too much.

Bacilar

To joke. To fool around.

Ex.

No te enojes, solo estaba vacilando. | Don't get mad, I was just joking.

Apañar

To take something for oneself so that other people may not take it. Sometimes, it means to steal something.

Ex.

Andaban dando tacos gratis, y me apañé un chingo para que cenemos juntos. | They were giving free tacos, and I took a bunch, so we can have dinner together.

Mear

To urinate. You can turn this verb into a noun and you would get "meados" which means "urine".

Ex.

Estoy enfermo, me duele cuando voy a mear. — I'm sick. It hurts when I pee.

Pichar

To pay for something that you and your whole gang of friends are going to use, drink, or eat. People also use "tirar" for the same meaning.

Ex.

Picha unas caguamas, güey. — Buy some 40oz. beers dude

Ningunear

To treat someone like shit, to not take someone into consideration or to humiliate someone. It comes from the adjective *"ninguno"* which means "no one".

Ex.

Tu hija tiene baja autoestima, porque siempre la ninguneas en las fiestas. — Your daughter has low self-esteem, because you always treat her like shit at parties.

Chamaquear

To fool or to take advantage of someone. It comes from the word *"chamaco"*, which means "young kid", so *chamaquear* implies that someone tricked you as if you were a naïve little kid.

Ex.

Te chamaquearon, pagaste demasiado por ese auto. — They fooled you, you payed way too much for that car.

Amolarse

To endure something unpleasant. This one is an irregular verb of the type o -> ue. (The "o" in the middle changes to "ue" in all conjugations except "nosotros").

Ex.

Vas a comerte tus verduras y te amuelas. — You are going to eat your veggies. Deal with it!

Bajar

To steal someone's girlfriend (or just to steal something). Women also use this verb to imply that they are having their period. Outside the world of slang *Bajar* simply means to lower something or to go down.

Ex.

El conductor de autobús me dio baje con la feria. — The bus driver stole my change.

Le voy a bajar su novia a ese — I'm going to steal that asshole's girlfriend.

cabrón.

No me ha bajado. Tengo miedo de estar embarazada.

I haven't had my period. I'm scared of being pregnant.

Paletear

To be very braggy, about stuff you do or have. Someone who brags a lot is called a *paletoso*. It comes from the word "*paletea*" which means lollipop.

Ex.

No salí con él, porque siempre presumía, y no me gustan los hombres paletosos.

I didn't go out with him, because he was always showing off, and I don't like men that brag.

Balconear

To tell and uncover secrets about someone, without their permission, exposing them. It comes from the word "*Balcón*", which means balcony.

Quemar (to burn) it's used in the exact same way. An English equivalent of these verbs would be "To spill the beans".

Ex.

Su mejor amiga la balconeó accidentalmente. Le preguntó a sus papás cuántos meses tenía

Her best friend spilled the beans by accident. She asked her parents how many months *de embarazo y ellos no sabían que su hija estaba embarazada.* — she had of pregnancy and they didn't even know that their daughter was pregnant.

Batear

To reject someone romantically or sexually. In regular Spanish, *batear* means to hit something with a bat.

Ex.

Creí que le gustaba, pero al final me bateó. — I thought she liked me, but in the end, she rejected me.

Terapear

To persuade someone. It comes from the word *terapia* which means therapy.

Ex.

Tu ex te está terapeando. No dejes que te manipule. — Your ex is persuading you. Don't let him manipulate you.

Sangrar

To take financial advantage of someone. The literal meaning of this verb is "To bleed". In this context, money is the blood of a person and you're making that person bleed out.

Ex.

Quiero ser independiente, y dejar de sangrar a mi padre.	I want to be independent, and stop taking money from my father.

Cantinflear

To talk gibberish, to babble or to talk in circles. It comes from Cantinflas, a Mexican comedian who was famous for talking in circles and giving rambling speeches in his movies. Because of that, we made a verb out of him.

Ex.

Cuando hablo en público, me pongo nervioso, y a veces cantinfleo.	When I speak in public, I get nervous, and I start to babble.

Jinetear

To avoid giving money for something someone's involved in. It could be a party or a project. The literal meaning of this word is "to ride a horse". In this sense, this person is riding over what other people contributed. In other words, to enjoy something that other people paid for. People who often do this are called "*Jinetes*".

Ex.

Cuando no tengo dinero, mis amigos pagan la peda, pero me siento mal por andar jineteando.

When I have no money, my friends pay for the boost, but I feel bad for not giving them any money.

Catafixiar

To exchange something. Everything seems to indicate that this term was invented by "Chabelo", the host of a long running Mexican children tv show where kids participated on many games to win prizes.

At the end of every show, the *Catafixia* took place. In this final challenge, the children had to choose between keeping all the prizes they had won so far, or exchanging them for a secret prize, which could be something way better than what they already had or way worst.

Ex.

Te catafixio unas cheves por unos cigarros.

Give me some cigarettes and I'll give you some of my beers.

Pelar

To notice someone/something, or to pay attention to someone/something.

Ex.

Le gustas a esa chava y tú ni la pelas. — That girl has a crush on you and you don't even notice her.

Outside slang, the verb "*pelar*" only means to peel a fruit or a vegetable, but it has abundant variations in Mexislang as we will see next.

Pelarse

To run away, to get away or to escape.

Ex.

El taxista atropelló a la ancianita y se peló. — The taxi driver ran over the old lady and got away.

Pelársela

To lose or to fail.

Ex.

Mi equipo se la peló otra vez. — My team lost again.

Intenté conseguir boletos para el concierto, pero me la pelé. — I tried to buy tickets for the concert, but I failed.

Que alguien te la pele

To defeat someone or to affirm that you're better than someone. This is actually a very disrespectful phrase and can spark up a fight.

Ex.

Llegué primero a la línea de meta antes que tú. Me la pelas.	I arrived at the finishing line before you. I beat you.
Tu novio me la pela.	I'm better than your boyfriend.

Rajar

To rat on someone or to give someone away.

Ex.

Interrogaron a Emilio por tres horas, pero él nunca rajó.	They interrogated Emilio for three hours, but he never ratted on anyone.

Rajarse

To back down on something you stated or promised. "Rajón", is someone who usually backs down a lot. It's also used to tease someone when he said he was going to do something, and now doesn't want to.

Ex.

No hagas planes con él. Al final siempre se raja.

Don't make plans with him. He always backs down at the end.

Guacarearse

To puke or to throw up. The not-slang verb for this is "*vomitar*".

Ex.

Bebí mucha cerveza y me guacarié.

I drank way too much beer, and I puked.

Chulear

To praise something or someone.

You call someone "chulo", or "chula", if you find them good looking or pretty.

Ex.

En la fiesta, me chulearon mucho mi vestido.

At the party, they praised my dress a lot.

Tu hermana está muy chula. ¡Preséntamela!

Your sister is really cute. Introduce me to her!

Bañársela

To do something outrageous or to go too far. You can also use the verbs "Pasársela" or "Mamársela" with the same effect.

Ex.

Te la bañaste insultando a la maestra enfrente de toda la clase. You went too far insulting the teacher in front of the whole class.

Castrar

To annoy someone. Literally, it means to remove the genitals of a male.

Ex.

Deja de estar castrando.   Stop being so annoying.

Pandear

To chicken out or to not attend to a social gathering. When someone doesn't go to a party, or event you invited him, you call him a "*pander*" or you say he "*pandeo*" to complain about his absence.

Ex.

El otro día pandeaste. ¿Qué   You failed us that other day by not coming. What happened?

pasó?

Sordear

To play dumb. It comes from the word "*sordo*" which means deaf. Literally *sordear* could be translated as "to pretend like you are deaf".

Ex.

| *Se está sordeando, sabe que su exnovia está aquí en la fiesta con otro hombre.* | He's playing dumb, he knows his ex is here at the party with another man. |
| *La saludé en el supermercado, pero se sordeó, e hizo como si no me vio.* | I said hi to her in the supermarket, but she played dumb, and pretended like she didn't see me. |

Jalar

To lift weights. To attend a social gathering or to express that a device is working correctly. Outside the world of slang, this verb only means "to pull".

Ex.

| *Él está en buena forma porque ya lleva jalando varios meses.* | He is in good shape because he's been lifting weights for a few months already. |

Mi hermano va a jalar a la fiesta. My brother is coming to the party.

Este celular tiene más de diez años y todavía jala. This cellphone is more than ten years old and it's still working.

Machetear

To read and reread something until you learn it or memorize it. To study very hard.

Example:

Saca buenas calificaciones por que siempre esta macheteando.

He gets good grades because he is always studying really hard.

Chapter 5
Mexislang words

I tried to make everything as clear as possible while writing this book, because the main problem I see, even with advanced Spanish students, is that they don't learn these kind of words at school or books, and even if their grammar is perfect, they usually have trouble when they have to interact with real people.

This is the longest chapter of the book, as it contains single noun and expressions in Mexican slang that just don't fit in any of the other categories, and because there's a bunch of them, this is probably the chapter that you will recheck the most.

As always, this contains examples and explanations on every word and expression and sometimes the story behind them.

Chafa

It means something is cheaply made, of inferior quality, or an imitation of a branded product.

Ex.

Este carro está muy chafa. Se ha descompuesto dos veces desde que lo compré, y eso fue hace un mes.

This car sucks. It has broken down twice since I bought it, and that was a month ago.

Gringo

This is a word you must already know, if you are an American. *Gringo* is the slang word Mexicans use to refer to people from the US. It is not meant to be an insult or to be derogatory. There's many colorful myths about the origin of this word. One of them states that during the Mexican American war from 1846-1848, the American government sent a battalion composed of mostly Irish-American immigrant soldiers to invade and fight against Mexico. However, during this invasion, the perspective of the Irish-Americans drastically changed when they realized that Mexico was mostly a Catholic country such as their native Ireland. They began to question why they were invading a Catholic country on behalf of the US, which was mostly a Protestant nation. Because of this, the battalion decided to defect the US Army and join the Mexican forces, fighting against the Americans. They were known as the Saint Patrick Battalion or *"Batallón de San Patricio"* and one of the main songs they used to chant when they were marching was "Green Grow the Rushes, O". Upon hearing this song multiple times, the Mexicans began to call them *"Gringos"* because that's what they understood from the lyrics when they chanted "Green Grow". Note that this is just one origin story out of many. Nowadays the term has evolved to refer to Americans in general, not just Irish-Americans. Mexicans are usually pretty bad at distinguishing between Americans, Canadians and Europeans. So, if you're Canadian or European and someone calls you a "gringo", please don't take it as an insult, chances are that the person just did it by accident. Mexicans also use the word "gringo" to refer to something that was made in the US.

Ex.

Se fue a Estados Unidos y se casó con un gringo.	She went to the US and she married an American.
-Oye, ya llevas años con esa computadora y todavía jala.	-Hey, you have had that computer for years and it's still working.
-Pues claro, mi compu es gringa, no como la tuya que es china.	-Of course, it was made in the US, not like yours which was made in China.

Chavo/Morro/Ruco

"*Chavo/chava*", is the slang way to refer to an unknown young man or woman. It isn't disrespectful nor vulgar, it's a very playful word that you can use in front of anyone. The same with "*morro/huerco/chamaco*", but with smaller children, and the slang word for old people is "*ruco/ruca*", but this one is a little stronger, and some might find it disrespectful to call and elder this way. It's mostly used by young people to talk about older people when they are not around.

Some men also can call *"mi ruca /mi vieja"* (old lady) to their girlfriend when they are with their friends.

Lately, people on the internet created the term "*chavorruco*", a mix of the terms *chavo* and *ruco* to refer to full grown adults (in their late 30s or 40s) that behave or dress like teenagers or young people. While it's kind of silly, it's worth mentioning because if you travel to Mexico, you may hear this.

Ex.

El morro/huerco corre por el parque.	The small child runs through the park.
Esa chava es muy bonita.	That girl is really pretty.
Mi ruca me abandonó.	My girl left me.
Ese ruco siempre está enojado.	That old man is always angry.
Mi hermano tiene 37 años y sale de fiesta con mis compañeros de la universidad. Es un chavorruco.	My brother is 37 years old and he goes out to party with my college classmates. He is a manchild.

Gato

Of course, it literally means cat, but in Mexislang it's a very derogatory way to refer to a servant, or a helper, or someone you send to do errands for you.

Ex.

Dile a tu gato que nos traiga unos cigarros.	Tell your servant to go get some cigarettes for us.

Fresa

In normal Spanish, *fresa* means strawberry, but in Mexican slang, it means someone is snobby or stuck up, or they only like people and things they think are of high quality. It's the opposite of *naco*.

Ex.

No salgas con esa chica, es muy fresa.

Don't date that girl, she is very snobby.

Naco

We say someone is a "naco/naca", when a person has bad taste, bad manners and/or a lack of education. "Redneck" is the most similar word I can think of in the English language that resembles the meaning of *Naco*.

It's often used by people of higer social status to talk about the things they think are beneath them or they would never do.

Ex.

-Me encanta mezclar whisky con Coca.

-¡Qué naco eres!

-I love to mix whisky with coke.

-You have such bad taste!

¡Aguas!

Agua means water, but "¡aguas!" is a quick way to warn someone about something dangerous. It is the Mexican slang way to say watch out, or beware. From this, another expression derives: "Echar aguas", which means to assist a driver when they are trying to park, and they don't have good visibility which may cause them to hit another car.

Ex.

¡Aguas!	Watch out!
¡Aguas con el perro!	Beware of the dog!
Quiero salir de reversa, pero ese carro está muy cerca de mí. Échame aguas, por favor.	I want to exit in reverse, but that car is too close by. Could you assist me, please?

Aza/Azo/Ala

These three are expressions of surprise most of the time, but can also express discomfort, fear, excitement, etc. They can be used as both positive and negative statements, and are usually said along with words like "mecha" "verga" "madre" "puta madre" "máquina" to accentuate the intensity of the emotion, even though they can be used alone and by themselves.

Ex.

¡Azo madre! Esto es demasiada comida.	Damn! This is way too much food.
Ala verga, güey ¡estás bien pendejo!	Holy fuck, dude, you're such a dumbass!
Aza mecha, güey, gracias. Qué buen regalo.	Holy crap dude! thank you. What a nice gift.

Chamba

Slang for "work". People from Mexico are hard workers so you will hear them say this word a lot. It can also be used as a verb "*chambear*". When it's a small, easy-to-do job, people refer to it as "*chambita*", however, when they're talking about a big, difficult or exhausting job, they tend to call it "*chinga*".

Instead of "*chamba*" people also may use the word "*jale*". These two terms are synonyms in the world of Mexislang.

Ex.

Tengo dinero para salir de fiesta, porque le hice unas chambitas a mi tío.	I have money to go out, because I did some small jobs for my uncle.
Ahora ya es casi imposible encontrar una buena chamba /	Nowadays it's almost impossible to find a good job.

un buen jale.

Ese trabajo es una chinga. Te tienes que levantar a las 4 de la mañana.	That job is brutal. You have to wake up at 4:00 AM.

Carnal

"Brother", the original meaning of the word refers to something related to the human flesh, in slang, this word is used to refer to a brother or a very close friend. It's also used when a stranger wants to be friendly, or wants to make himself look more truthful to someone he just met.

Ex.

Mi carnal tiene 20 años.	My brother is 20 years old.
¿Qué pedo carnal?	What's up bro?

Chesco

"Soda" usually a Coke.

Ex:

Cómprame un chesco güey, te	Buy me a soda dude, I'll pay you tomorrow.

lo pago mañana.

Lana/varo/feria

All of them refer to money. Literally "*Lana*" means wool and it's slang for money in general. "*Feria*" means pocket change or coins. From it, we have derived the verb "*ferear*" which means to exchange a big bill for its same value but in coins. "*Varo*" is used instead of peso to express the Mexican currency.

Ex.

-¿Puedes pagar la cuenta?	-Can you pay the bill?
-No traigo lana.	-I don't have any money
¡Esa madre cuesta veinte mil varos!	¡That thing costs twenty thousand pesos!
¿Tienes feria?	Do you have pocket change?

Hueva

"Laziness", from it, we get the adjective of *huevón* or *huevona*, which means a lazy person. As we have already seen, *huevo* tends to be used as a slang term to refer to testicles. The term *huevón* comes from the notion that someone has very heavy testicles and they don't allow him to move as much as he could. That's sort of the idea.

Outside the world of slang, the term *hueva* actually means "fishroe".

Ex.

Tengo hueva de ir al trabajo	I'm feeling lazy about going to work.
Ese cabrón es bien huevón. Nunca hace nada.	That asshole is so lazy. He never does anything.

Vato

Another form of saying "dude". It can easily be exchanged with "*güey*".

Ex.

¿Qué onda vato?	Whats up dude?

Orale

It has many different meanings depending on the context.

It can be used to express agreement and affirmation.

Ex.

-*Te veré mañana a las 5:00 AM.*	-I'll see you tomorrow at 5:00 AM.

- *Órale carnal.*   -Sure bro.

It can be used to tell someone to hurry up.

Ex.

Órale, tengo prisa.   Hurry up, I'm in a rush.

It can be used to express surprise.

Ex.

¡Órale! Qué comida tan sabrosa.   Wow! What a delicious meal!

It can also be used to express that you are not happy with something someone is doing, and you want them to stop.

Ex.

¡Órale, cabrón! Ya deja de andar inventando rumores de mi hermana.   That's enough, asshole! Stop spreading false rumors about my sister.

MEXISLANG   RAÚL JIMÉNEZ

Ules, Oles, Eles and Ales

These are a few words of slang that come from "*órale*" but have a variety of meanings.

Híjole: It's like saying jeez, or yikes in English. It can also mean "damn", depending on the context. It expresses feelings of surprise, frustration and/or shock, depending on when it's used.

Ex.

¡Híjole! ¡No esperaba verte aquí!	I wasn't expecting to see you here.
¡Híjole!, ya es muy tarde y no termino mi trabajo.	Damn! It's late and I haven't finished my work.

Ándale: Speedy González catchphrase. It usually means hurry up, but it can also mean you agree with something or it's also used when you are trying to convince someone.

Ex.

Ándale, ya cámbiate para irnos.	Hurry up! Change clothes so we can go
Ándale, así sí me gusta la foto.	Now this way I like the picture more.
-Vamos a Cancún.	-Let's go to Cancun.
-No tengo ganas.	-I don't want to.
-Ándale, no seas aburrido.	-Come on, don't be boring.

Éjele: This is what you say when you catch someone doing something he shouldn't be doing, but in a playful way.

Ex.

¡Éjele! Te ví besándote con la hija del jefe. No te hagas sordo.	Hey! I saw you kissing the boss's daughter. Don't play dumb.

Épale: You said this when someone is doing something you don't want to. It means stop, but it doesn't translate to stop. When you use "épale", you must state right after why you are not comfortable with what the other person is doing.

Ex.

¡Épale! Esos tacos son míos.	Hey stop! Those tacos are mine.

Quihúbole: It means Hi, or What's up?

Ex.

Quihúbole carnal, ¿cómo has estado?	What's up bro, how are you doing?

Újule: It express disappointment in something or someone.

Ex.

Újule, ni estuvo tan buena la peli.	Bummer, the movie wasn't even that good

Húchale: it means you are very disappointed. Like a heavier version of *újule*

Ex.

Húchale. Perdieron el partido después de que estaban ganando.

Damn. They lost the match after having the upper hand.

Malinchista

In order to understand this term, first you have to know who the "Malinche" was.

La Malinche was an Aztec woman who lived during the time of the Spanish Invasion in Mexico. She was offered as a slave to Hernan Cortez (the leader of the Spanish Occupation). After spending some time with the Spaniards, la Malinche learned Spanish quickly and she became a spanish-nahuatl interpreter working for Cortez. She eventually became his mistress and advisor. The contributions that she did for the Spaniards proved essential for the Spanish conquest of Mexico and the fall of the Aztec Empire.

Because of this, la Malinche is seen as the ultimate symbol of national betrayal. Her character gave birth to the term "malinchista", which means "a Mexican that prefers foreign things". There really isn't an English equivalent to this.

Ex.

-Yo solo escucho música en inglés.

-I only listen to music in English.

-No seas malinchista, escucha música mexicana también. — -Don't be malinchista, you should listen to Mexican music also.

Bronca

A serious problem or something troublesome, it could also mean a fight or a conflict.

Ex.

¿Puedes ayudarme? Tengo una bronca. — Can you help me? I have a problem.

Resolver estos ejercicios de matemáticas es una bronca. — Answering these math exercises is a pain.

No quiero que haya broncas entre nosotros. — I don't want there to be conflict between us.

Hubo bronca en la fiesta de ayer. — There was a fight at yesterday's party.

Paro

A favor. From it, we derive the phrase "*hacer el paro*", which means to do a favor. It's very informal, of course. So, just use it when you want to ask a person you know well to do you a favor.

Ex.

Hazme el paro para tener una — Help me to get a date with your sister, please.

cita con tu hermana, porfa.	Teacher, help me out, please. Could you assign me an extra-credit project to pass the class?
Profe, hágame el paro. Póngame un trabajo con puntos extra para aprobar.	

Tianguis

A *tianguis*, or *rodante* are the names given to street markets in Mexican slang. These are very colorful places that take over the whole street and sell all kinds of stuff, like low quality Chinese/Mexican ripoff toys, used clothes, pirated CDs and DVDs, but also fruits, meat, spices, exotic remedies and whatever you can imagine.

Here, you'll hear a lot of noise, including: "cumbia" and "banda "music in the background, and sellers yelling at people walking by, trying to sell their products. They call "*marchante*" to the costumers, because they are "marching" through the streets seeing all the stuff on sale.

There's some *rodantes* that have schedules, and move from place to place within a city depending on the day, and some that are always in the same place, like the most famous one, *Tepito* on downtown Mexico City.

Ex.

Ve a comprar fruta al tianguis.	Go buy some fruit at the street market.

Neta

The truth.

Ex.

¡Es neta, güey! ¡Yo no lo hice! — It's the truth, dude. I didn't do it.

¿Es neta? — For real?

Jefe/Jefa

Dad or mom. Of course, "jefe" actually means boss, but we also nickname our parents in that way because they always represent an authority figure.

Ex.

Vamos al cotorreo. Mi jefa va a cuidar a mi hijo. — Let's go to party. My mom is going to take care of my son.

Reta

A friendly match. It's usually a soccer match among friends, but it could be of any other sport, or even videogames.

Ex.

En ese parque se arman las retas. — In that park they play friendly matches.

¿Jalas a las retas de básquet? — Are you coming to play a few matches of basketball?

Troca

Truck and it's actually a deformation of this English word. The proper word in Spanish is "*camioneta*".

Ex.

Quiero comprar una troca nueva. — I want to buy a new truck.

Cantón

One's own house or "my place".

Vamos a mi cantón. — Let's go to my place.

Cuate

Friend. You can also use "*compa*" or "*camarada*". "*Cuate*" means twin in regular Spanish.

Ex.

Hoy voy a salir con mis cuates. — Today I'll go out with my friends.

Canijo

A clever person or a challenging task to accomplish.

Ese boxeador es muy canijo, tiene buena estrategia.
That boxer is very clever, he has good tactics.

Está muy canijo hacer ejercicio todos los días, y además trabajar, cocinar y cuidar a mis tres hijos.
It's very hard to exercise every day, besides working, cooking, doing chores and taking care of my 3 children.

Gacho

"Not cool", "bad" "mean" or "unpleasant", it's the opposite of *chido*.

Ex.

Está muy gacho el clima.
The weather is very unpleasant.

Házme el paro, no seas gacho.
Help me out, don't be mean.

Está muy gacha la comida en este restaurante.
Food sucks in this restaurant.

Está muy gacho tu novio.
Your boyfriend is very ugly.

Ardido

To be resentful about something. It comes from the verb "arder" which means to sting.

People also may use "*ardilla*" (squirrell), because it sounds very similar, and it express the same thing.

Ex.

Tu exnovia quedó muy ardida cuando la dejaste.   Your ex-girlfriend became really resentful when you left her.

Ratero

Thief. Some may even call thieves *ratas* (rats)

Ex.

Deja eso allí, no seas ratero.   Leave that thing there, don't be a thief.

Chilango

Someone who was born and raised in Mexico City. They have a very particular accent that makes them stand out from other Mexicans. You can search for "chilango accent" on YouTube to hear it by yourself or you can also listen to the song "Chilanga banda" by Café Tacuba. All of the lyrics of the song are sang with a "chilango" accent.

Ex.

Supe que era chilango al momento en que empezó a hablar. — I knew that he was from Mexico City the moment he began to talk.

Codo

A stingy person. Someone who doesn't like to spend money. It literally means "elbow". "Me duele el codo" (My elbow hurts), it's an expression we use when we would like to buy something, but we are feeling stingy about it.

Ex.

Necesito comprar una nueva computadora, pero me duele el codo. — I need to buy a new computer, but I'm feeling stingy about it.

No salgas con ese hombre, es muy codo. — Don't date that man. He is very stingy.

Guácala

Expression of disgust. It's the equivalent of saying "yuck", "yikes" or "eww". People also tend to say "fuchi" or "fuchila" with the same meaning.

Ex.

-Te traje unos tacos — -I brought you Tacos

-Guácala, tienen aguacate. — -Yuck. It has avocado. I hate

Odio el aguacate.   avocado.

Betabel

An old person. It literally means beet. In normal Spanish, *betabel* means beet.

Ex.

Mi abuelo ya está betabel, tiene casi 90 años.   My grandfather is really old, he is almost 90 years old.

Vago

It has different meanings depending on the context. It can mean someone who likes to be out of his house a lot. It also can mean someone who is very skilled at some task. It's also a way to refer to a mischievous and playful kid or person. It comes from the verb "vagar", which means "to wander"

Ex.

Mi hermana anda de vaga con su novio todos los días.   My sister is out with her boyfriend every day.

Eres bien vago para este juego.   You are very good at this game.

Ese niño es muy vago.   That kid is very playful and mischievous.

Coyote

A nap. From it, we have the phrase "*Echar un coyote*" which means "To take a nap".

Ex.

| *Estoy cansado. Voy a echarme un coyotito.* | I'm tired. I'm going to take a short nap. |

Fusca

Handgun.

Ex.

| *Murió de un balazo, pero nunca encontraron la fusca.* | He died from a gunshot, but they never found the handgun. |

Mamache

This word is used in the expression "Llevar a mamache", which means to give someone a piggyback ride.

Ex.

| *Mi hijo se cansó de caminar, y lo llevé a mamache.* | My son got tired of walking, so I gave him a piggyback ride. |

Pata

Foot or feet. From it we have the phrases "a pata" which means "by foot" or "meter la pata" which means to screw up something by accident.

Ex.

Te apestan las patas.	Your feet smell bad.
Mi carro se descompuso, y tuve que regresar a mi casa a pata.	My car broke down, so I had to get back to my house walking.
Metí la pata con el examen.	I screwed up the test.

Ñoño

Nerd.

Ex.

En los 80s, solo los ñoños iban a la Comic-Con.	In the 80s, only nerds went to Comic-Con.

Mordida

A bribe.

Ex.

Si no hubiera pagado mordida, If I hadn't paid a bribe, the officer would have taken my *el oficial se habría llevado mi carro.* / car.

Tocayo

Someone who has the same name as you.

Ex.

Hay tres Lauras en mi clase de literatura, somos tocayas. / There's 3 Lauras in my literature class. We share the same name.

Piocha

To be very good or skillfull at some task. People also use "pirinola" which has the same meaning.

Ex.

Mi tío es una pirinola tocando guitarra. / My uncle is very skilled at playing guitar.

Mojón

A turd.

Ex.

Pisé un mojón cuando venía / I stepped on a turd on my way *hacia acá.*   here.

Jeta

Face.

Ex.

Hoy no quiero verte la jeta.   I don't want to see your face today.

Chompa

Head. People can also use other words like "*choya*", "*tatema*" or "*maceta*".

Ex.

Me duele la chompa.   I have a headache.

Plomazo

The sound of a gunshot.

Ex.

No salgas, escuchamos unos plomazos hace rato.   Don't go outside, we heard some gunshots a while ago.

Gandalla

Someone who takes advantage of a situation, or of other people. The verb form of this noun is "agandallar".

Ex.

Tu hermano es bien gandalla, siempre que viene se come toda nuestra comida. — Your brother always takes advantage of us, when he comes, he always eats all our food.

Machín

It comes from "macho", and "macho" means male. It has different meanings depending on the context.

It could be someone who is very manly.

Someone who is a close friend of yours.

Something kicks ass.

Another way of saying "a lot".

Ex.

Yo nunca lloro en las películas. Soy bien machín. — Movies never make me cry. I'm really manly.

¿Qué pedo, machín? ¿Cómo — What's up dude? How are you?

estás?

Tu carro está bien machín. — Your car kicks ass.

Me duele el estómago bien machín. — My stomach hurts a lot.

Cascarita

A street soccer match. Very informal, without rules, just for fun. Literally "*cáscara*" means peel, like a banana peel.

Ex.

Jugaremos una cascarita saliendo de la escuela. — We'll play a street soccer match after school.

Mojado

A wetback. A Mexican illegal immigrat living in the US. Literally, it means "a wet person".

Ex.

Lo deportaron después de estar de mojado por diez años. — He was deported after being a wetback for 10 years.

Pollero

Clandestine guides that help Mexican illegal immigrants to cross the border. Literally, it means "chicken seller".

Ex.

Interceptaron un camión de dulces, con muchos latinos adentro. Los arrestaron a ellos y a los polleros.	A candy truck with many latinos inside was intercepted. They were arrested, as well as the ones who organized the whole thing.

Simón

Very informal way of saying "yes".

Ex.

Simón, voy a hacer lo que dice.	Yes, I'm going to do what he says.

Nel

Very informal way to say "no". It's not used for constructing sentences. You can't say "Nel iré" instead of "no iré" (I won't go). It's used to just answer "no" mostly. Some people also say "naranjas" instead of no, and it's used the same way as "nel".

Ex.

-¿Quieres salir a comer?

-Nel.

-Do you want to go out to eat.
-Nah.

Chacha

A very derogatory way to call maids in México. You should never call your maid like this. It's very disrespectful but you may hear it when you listen other people talking about their maids.

Sometimes people say "*chacha*" to girls, to make them feel bad, implying they are low class, or servants.

Ex.

La chacha le puso cloro a mi vestido, y lo decoloró.

The maid used bleach on my dress and it lost its color.

Fulano/Fulana

An unknown man or an unknown woman. You can used this when you don't care, or don't know, or don't want to think about the names of the people you are talking about, or when you are talking about some hypothetical, like a John Doe. People also may use: "mengano, mengana, perengano, perengana, zutano, zutana".

Ex.

¿Quién es ese fulano?	Who is that guy?
Unas fulanas tocaron mi puerta.	Some women knocked on my door.
Si un fulano me quisiera enamorar, ¿qué harías?	If a man tried to make me fall in love with him, what would you do?

Barco

An easy to please teacher. If you have a teacher who is a "*barco*" you will pass his class without doing much effort. It's the complete opposite of a strict teacher. In regular Spanish, it means "ship".

Ex.

Tu promedio es alto porque siempre agarraste maestros barcos.	Your school grades are high because you always had easy teachers.

Guachicol

Stolen gasoline. In Mexico, gasoline is very overpriced because there's only one company allowed to sell it. That company is called Pemex (Petróleos Mexicanos) and they tend to overprice the fuel to make more money. Sometimes gasoline is just too expensive, and this has led to a group of criminals to start stealing it and selling it at cheaper prices, they are called "*Guachicoleros*".

Ex.

No tengo mucho varo. Tal vez tenga que comprar guachicol. I don't have much money. I may have to buy stolen gasoline.

Cariñoso

Expensive. In regular Spanish, this actually means "tender" but we change the meaning in slang because *caro* (expensive) and *cariñoso* sound similar, as they share the same first three letters.

Ex.

Quiero irme de viaje pero los hoteles están cariñosos. I want to go on a trip, but hotels are expensive.

Baboso

Dumbass. "*Baba*" means drool, "*baboso*" literally means drooler but in slang, we always use it with the meaning of dumbass or idiot.

Ex.

La cagaste. Estás bien baboso. You screwed up. You are such a dumbass.

Matado

Someone who puts a lot of effort on having good grades and studying. People can also say "matadito". It literally means "killed".

Ex.

Prefiero reprobar a andar de matadito estudiando. — I'd rather fail than to be studying like a maniac.

La banda

Group of friends. It literally means the band or the gang.

Ex.

Invité a toda la banda a cotorrear. — I invited the whole gang to party.

Cachirul

An illegal participant of a competition. Like a man dressing as a woman in a female soccer match, or someone beyond the age limit.

Ex.

Todos los de tu equipo se ven muy grandes. No vale jugar con cachirules. — All people in your team look older. You can't participate with players whose age breaks the rules.

Sobres

Expression to indicate you accept something or you are ok with something. People may also use "sale" or "vale".

Ex.

-*Nos vemos mañana en el parque.*

-*¡Sobres!*

-See you tomorrow by the park.

-Sure!

Aventón

A ride or a lift. It comes from the verb "aventar" which means "to throw".

Ex.

Si vas a tu casa, dame un aventón. Mi novia vive cerca.

If you're going to your house, give me a ride. My girlfriend lives nearby.

Llevado

Someone who is very indiscreet and its constantly playing mean jokes on people. When two people get along doing this kind of stuff with each other, you say they are "*llevados*" or "*así se llevan*" (that's how they treat each other).

Ex.

No invites a tu primo, no me agrada porque es bien llevado.

Don't invite your cousin. I don't like him, because he is very mean and indiscreet.

Chivas

Things. Literally it means "female goats".

Ex.

Dejé mis chivas en tu casa. Tráemelas.

I left my things at your house. Bring them to me.

El sope

Armpit. A "sope" is also a traditional Mexican dish in which a tortilla gets filled with food on top.

Ex.

Este desodorante me causa

This deodorant makes my armpit itch.

comezón en el sope.

Cursi

Corny, or cheesy.

Ex.

Mi novio es demasiado cursi. Es lindo, pero a veces puede llegar a ser molesto.

My boyfriend is way too chessy. That's cute, but, it can be annoying sometimes.

Zafo

Zafo is an expression you use when your group must perform a task but you personally, don't want to do it. It's like a way of saying "Not me".

Ex.

- ¡Alguien tiene que lavar los trastes!

-¡Zafo!

- Someone has to wash the dishes!

-Not me!

Acordeón

It's a little piece of paper where you write all the answers of a test and use it to cheat. It is called that way because people usually fold it in a shape resembling an accordion.

Ex.

Pasé todos mis exámenes gracias a mi acordeón.   I passed all my tests thanks to my hidden cheating paper.

Trucha

To pay attention or to beware. Other ways to express the same are "estar/ponerse al tiro", "estar/ponerse al cien" "al cien". Literally, it means "trout fish".

Ex.

Trucha con los policías.   Beware of the policemen.

Pelado

A rude or disrespectful person. You can also say "*pelado*" to refer to a random man you don't know by name.

Ex.

Dejé de juntarme con él, porque era un pelado. — I stop hanging out with him because he was very disrespectful.

Me gusta ese pelado. — I like that man.

Gallo

It literally means rooster. In Mexican slang, "gallo" has different meanings depending of the context.

It can be used to express that moment when someone is singing and goes out of tune making a weird squeaky sound. It can also be used to express someone who is very good at something (ser buen gallo), or that someone is your most trusted or favorite person. It can also be used, when you have the flu, to talk about phlegms, or to provoke someone who thinks too much of himself and has a lot of nerve (¿muy gallito?).

Ex.

De niño cantaba muy bien, pero cuando se hizo adolescente, cambió su voz y le salían muchos gallos. — As a child he sang very good, but when he became a teen, his voice changed, and went out of tune often.

Mi amigo practica artes marciales, y es muy buen gallo. — My friend practices martial arts, and he is great at it.

De todos los que participan en — Of all the tournament participants, you are the best *el torneo, tú eres mi gallo.* | one (or my favorite).

No dejo de aventar gallos por esta gripa. | I can't stop coughing out phelgms because of this flu.

Eres muy gallito, pero eso te mete en problemas innecesarios. | You got a lot of guts/nerve, but that gets you into unnecessary trouble.

Guapachoso

Happy and dancing people or music. It's often used when talking about Latino centric dance music genres, like cumbia, or salsa, instead of disco, electronic or dance music.

Ex.

No puedo evitar bailar cuando escucho un ritmo guapachoso. | I can't help but to dance when I hear a dancy rhythm.

Puñetas

Fragile or weak. People may also say "ñetas".

Ex.

Si te peleas con el novio de tu ex, te va a matar. Estás bien puñetas. | If you fight your ex-girlfriend's new boyfriend, he'll kill you. You are super weak.

Pitero

It comes from "*pito*" (slang for male genitalia), and it's used to say something, or someone is not very good, cheaply made or of low quality.

Ex.

Este encendedor ni prende, está bien pitero. This lighter doesn't even light up, it's cheaply made

Mono

Cute. It literally means monkey. It's more commonly used in Spanish from Spain, but it's also used enough in Mexican slang to mention it here.

Ex.

Este peluche está muy mono. That plushie is very cute.

Ñero

Someone with bad taste, or lack of education. Like *naco*, but worst.

Ex.

No me gustan los narcocorridos ni las cumbias, así que no pongas tu música de ñero. | I don't like narcocorridos nor cumbias, so don't play your distasteful music.

Barbero

Brown-noser or ass-kisser. It literally means "barber". People may also use "*lambiscón*" for the same meaning.

Ex.

Roberto anda de barbero con el jefe, porque quiere salir temprano. | Roberto is kissing the boss' ass, because he wants to leave work early.

Alcahuete

An overly permissive parent or teacher.

Ex.

Vamos a besarnos, el profesor es un alcahuete. | Let's kiss, the teacher is very permissive.

Tronco

An unskilled person or someone who is not agile nor physically fit. It literally means "wood log".

Ex.

Eres mi amigo, pero no te quiero en mi equipo, porque al chile, estás bien tronco.

You are my friend, but I don't want you on my team, because you aren't very skilled at this game.

Vientos

Another way of saying "ok" or "good". You can't form sentences with it. Literally, it means "winds" and it acquired this meaning in slang because the first syllable of "*vientos*" sounds identical to the word "*bien*".

Ex.

Mañana llega tu paquete.

Your package arrives tomorrow.

– Vientos.

- Ok.

Cámara

It's used to convey approval, and/or encouragement. In regular Spanish, it means camera, like a video or photo camera.

Ex.

Cámara.

It's ok.

Cámara, nos vemos.

Goodbye, have a good day.

Cámara, te toca — Cheer up/don't be afraid, it's your turn.

Cafre

A driver that drives very fast, without caution, and very propense to cause an accident.

Ex.

No te vayas con él. Es un cafre, y aparte anda pedo. — Don't go with him. He's a crazy driver, plus he's drunk.

Fantoche

Someone who is always showing off and is very annoying because of how much he does it.

Ex.

A nadie le cae bien Fernando, porque es un fantoche. — Nobody likes Fernando because he is a show off.

Valedor

A trusted friend. Someone who always has your back. It comes from "*valer*" which means "to worth".

Ex.

¿Como está mi valedor? — How is my most trusted fellow?

Fritangas

Excessively fried food. It comes from the verb "fritar", which means "to fry".

Ex

Si sigues comiendo fritangas vas a engordar. — If you keep eating fried food, you are going to get fat.

Chucherías

Junk food.

Ex.

La dieta no me deja comer chucherías. — My diet doesn't allow me to eat junk food.

Garnachas

Garnacha is usually a thick tortilla, fried and with food inside, but in Mexican slang, it's a general word used to call every corn made Mexican street food out there, like *gorditas, sopes, flautas, and migadas*.

Ex.

Las garnachas son deliciosas, pero no muy saludables. — Mexican corn-based street food is delicious, but not very healthy.

Chamuco

The devil.

Ex.

Actúa como loco. Parece que se le metió el chamuco.   He is acting crazy. It seems as if the devil took hold of him.

Chicano

Mexican Americans. Offsprings of Latin Americans parents that grew up in the US.

Ex.

No puedo hablar con mis primos, porque son chicanos y no saben español.   I can't talk with my cousins, because they grew up in the US, and they don't know Spanish.

Botana

The literal translation of this word, means "snacks", but its also used in mexislang to refer to something funny, or entretaining.

Ex.

Está bien botana este meme. This meme is very funny.

Compra algunas botanas para la fiesta. Buy some snacks for the party.

Chengo

Mexican slang for someone who dresses awful, and/or is very dirty.

Ex.

¡Arréglate! Estás muy chenga. Dress up! Your clothes/style is awful.

Chitón

Mexislang expression to tell someone to hush, or to keep a secret.

Ex.

Vamos por unos tacos, pero chitón. Se supone que estoy a dieta. Let's get some tacos, but dont tell anyone. I'm supposed to be on a diet.

Prieto

Despective way to call someone whos skin is kinda brownish, like the regular and steryotipical latino skin coloration.

Ex.

No me gustan los prietos. — I don't like guys with brown skin color.

Greña

Mexislang way to say hair.

Ex.

Tienes la greña muy larga. — You have very long hair.

Sobaco

Slang way to call an armpit. Another word with the same meaning, its "sope".

Ex.

Ponte desodorante. Te apesta el sope. — Put on some dehodorant. Your armpit smells bad.

Matasanos

Literally means "the ones who kill healthy people". This is a common slang to refer to a doctor, joking and teasing about a possible medical error.

Ex.

Mi Padre es un matasanos. — My dad is a doctor.

Guarura

Mexican slang for bodyguard.

Ex.

Ese hombre es importante, porque siempre tiene un guarura cerca.

That man is important, because he always has a bodyguard near him.

Equis

The way you pronounce "X" in Spanish. In Mexico it's used as an equivalent for "whatever".

Ex.

Equis wey, ya vamonos.

Whatever dude, let's go.

Todólogo:

The Mexican equivalent of the phrase: Jack of all trades.

Ex.

No tengo puesto fijo, soy todólogo. — I don't have a fixed job position. I'm a jack of all trades.

Choninos/chones:

Old Mexican slang for underwear.

Ex.

Se rompió tu pantalón y se te ven los choninos. — Your pants broke and your underwear is exposed.

Chapter 6
Party, drugs and alcohol
Mexislang words.

Clubbing and partying in Mexico is different depending on the city. Some cities have tons of nightclubs, while some others just have a few bars and cantinas, but no matter where you are, you'll always find a Mexican willing to party alongside you. Here is a list of Mexislang words for partying and to talk about alcohol and drugs. They can be useful to people looking to have fun going out at night in Mexico.

Antro

Nightclub. Going clubbing is usually called "antrear".

Ex.

| *Hoy no quiero ir al antro. Quiero quedarme a ver películas.* | I don't want to go to the club tonight. I want to stay and watch some movies. |

Perreo

A form of dancing in which a woman moves her buttocks rubbing the male genitalia while she dances. It's the Latin American word for Grinding, and while it comes from Puerto Rico and other countries from the south, it's used in all of Latin America.

Ex.

> *Vamos al antro, quiero perrear con una chica.* — Let's go to the club. I want to grind dance with a girl.

Rola

Song. People use "*rolón*" for a very good song.

Example

> *¿Cómo se llama esa rola?* — What's the name of that song?
>
> *¡Que rolón!* — What a kickass song!

Cotorrear

To socialize with people or to hangout. "*Cotorreo*" means party. Other words for party are: Peda, *Juerga, Reventón, Pachanga, Parranda.*

Ex.

Let's go to a party at my cousin's house.	Vamos al cotorreo en casa de mi primo
¿Cuándo es la pachanga?	When is the party?
Tengo prohibido tomar, no puedo salir de juerga.	I am not allowed to drink, I can't go out partying.
Estaba cotorreando con un amigo.	I was hanging out with a friend.

Chela

Beer. People may also say "*Cheve*".

Ex.

Tengo ganas de una chela bien fría.	I want to get a really cold beer.

Caguama

A 40 oz beer. They are fairly inexpensive in Mexico. People may also refer to them as "guamas". Literally "caguama" is the name of a big species of turtle.

Ex.

No tengo tanto dinero, pero podemos comprar unas caguamas. — I don't have much money, but we can buy a few 40 oz. beers.

Agualoca

An improvised and cheaply made alcoholic drink. In Mexican stores, you can find a very strong and pure alcohol, made from distilled sugarcane juice. It's very low quality and it's extremely cheap. For a little less than a dollar you can get a liter of it. Most of the times, the bottle isn't even made of glass, but from plastic. People tend to mix it with 15-20 liters of water, and cool–aid, tang or any other fruit-flavored powder. The name *agua loca* literally means "crazy water".

Ex.

Si no tienes dinero, y quieres emborracharte, haz agualoca. — If you don't have money, and want to get drunk, do some crazy water.

Pistear

Drinking alcohol. The word *Pisto* means alcohol, but it's mostly used to refer to beer.

Legends say this word comes from "pista de baile" (dance floor) because years ago, when Mexican youths went to dance, they also were drinking, and probably some hip and drunk kid who is now 40 plus years old thought it was cool to say that. Of course, nobody can know if this is true, but it's a fun story nonetheless.

Other Mexislang ways to refer to alcohol in general: El mame, el chupe

Other Mexislang ways to refer to the act of consuming alcohol: Mamar, Chupar

Ex.

Vamos a comprar pisto.	Let's go buy some beer.
Vamos a pistear.	Let's go drink alcohol.

Pomo

A bottle of alcohol, that isn't beer. Something like whisky vodka or tequila, for example.

Ex.

Hoy no quiero cheve. Vamos a comprar un pomo.	I don't want beer today. Let's buy a bottle of liqueur.

Mala copa

A person with a very over the top behavior after getting drunk. It could be aggressive, sad, noisy, or disrespectful, maybe even a combination of all.

People who cry, yell, annoy others, start doing weird dances or get into fights after drinking are considered to be "mala copa". It literally means "bad glass".

Puedes venir a la fiesta, pero no bebas, porque te pones de mala copa.	You can come to the party. Just don't drink, because nobody can stand.it when you get drunk.

Estar fumado

To be under the influence of drugs. You can also use "estar fumado" when someone says something ridiculous, or is doing something stupid, comparing his weird or uncommon actions with the ones of someone who is high.

Other nouns for being under the influence, or being someone who actively consumes drugs, are: *Chemo, Grifo, Pacheco.*

Ex.

Soy bien grifo	I do a lot of drugs.

Estoy Pacheco — I'm under the influence of drugs.

Mi amigo probo la marihuana una vez, y se puso bien chemo. — My friend tried marihuana once, and he got super high.

¿Estás fumado? El precio de tu producto es demasiado alto — Are you high? The price of your product is way too high.

Mota

Marijuana.

Outside slang. *Mota* is used to call a small ball of fabric that comes out of clothes.

Ex.

Ese vato es bien grifo. Todo el día está fumando mota. — That dude consumes a lot of drugs. He is smoking pot all day.

Churro

A joint. Outside the world of slang, a "churro" is a famous Spanish dessert. People may also use the word "churros" to describe curly hair. A bad movie is often also called a "churro".

Ex.

Vamos con ese güey, siempre tiene al menos un churro para — Let's hang out with that dude. He always has at least a joint to share.

compartir.

Tengo hambre, quiero comer churros.	I'm hungry, I want to eat some churros.
Me gustan las mujeres con muchos churros en su cabello.	I like girls with curly hair.
Fuimos al cine, y la película fue un churro.	We went to the movies and the flick sucked.

Tachas

Drug ecstasy. In school-related slang, *tachas* mean x marked mistakes in an exam or homework.

Ex.

Fui a una fiesta muy loca, donde había mucho alcohol, tachas y perico.	I went to the craziest party. There were tons of alcohol, ecstasy and cocaine.
Mi examen está lleno de tachas.	My exam is full of mistakes.

Perico

Cocaine. Other words for the same drug are *coca*, *nieve* (snow), *azúcar* (sugar), *pera* and *parluca*. In regular Spanish *"perico"* means parrot.

Ex.

Inhalé dos líneas de perico.   I inhaled two lines of cocaine.

Cruda

Hangover. Literally, it means raw.

Ex.

Ando bien crudo.   I'm hungover.

Quinceañera

A coming of age party done in Mexico and Latin America, to conmemorate a girl (who is also "la quinceañera") turned 15 years old. There are also male *quinceañeros*, but it's not very common.

Quinceañeras are huge parties that are considered events as big as a wedding, sometimes even bigger, and have many rituals, like going to church to receive a blessing, then dancing the waltz with her *chambelan*, the family and guests, plus some other coming of age party games, like gifting the girl her last doll, or a surprise gift from her friends. The usual dress color for *quinceañeras* is pink, but if she wants another color, she can wear it. It's the equivalent to a sweet sixteen party, but for fifteen year olds instead. People also say "*Una quiña*" in slang, to refer to the quinceañera party.

Ex.

Me invitaron a una quiña. | I was invited to a Latino sweet fifteen party.

Chambelán

The dancing partner (or partners) of the *quinceañera*, selected by her or by her family, to dance the Waltz with, and to escort her. *Chambelánes* are friends and/or cousins most of the time, and they practice the dance alongside the girl weeks or months before to prepare for the day of the party.

Ex.

No quiero ser tu chambelán, porque no me gusta bailar. | I don't want to be your sweet fifteen dancing partner, because I don't like dancing.

Chapter 7
Sex, sexuality and dating Mexislang words.

A good part of Mexican slang is about sex, dating, love, passion and infidelity. These are words that you'll probably need to at least know, if you are single and plan on staying in Mexico for a while.

Mexican people love to get in relationships (long and short term) with foreign people, and if you bond with them using the dialect they are familiar with, it may be easier to hook up with someone here, if that is your intention.

In this final Mexislang chapter, I compiled a list of all the sex and dating related Mexislang expressions and words I could find. You can use them to figure out what your Mexican partner is saying, to understand dirty jokes and double entendre or to know if someone is being disrespectful to you.

Mexislang ways to say penis

El camote (sweet potato)

La corneta (the cornet)

El chile (the chili pepper)

El garrote (the weapon, club)

La gaver (la verga with the order of the syllables inverted)

El nepe (El pene with the order of the syilabes inverted)

El gusano (the worm)

La herramienta (the tool)

El leño (the wooden log)

La macana (police stick)

La manguera (the hosepipe)

La ñonga

La vaina

La reata

El pito

La verga

El pepino (the cucumber).

Mexislang ways to say vagina

Most of these are very offensive, and are mostly said between males. The ones I've heard women use in conversation are *pucha* and *pepa*.

El bizcocho (biscuit)

La panocha

La concha (seashell)

El hachazo (ax cut)

La papaya

La pepa

La pucha

La rajada (cut)

Las verijas

El coño

El chocho

El sapo (frog)

La almeja (clam)

La rayita (little straight line)

El burro

La pantufla (the slipper)

Mexislang ways to say breasts

Las chimeneas (chimney)

Las chiches

Las mamilas (nipples)

Las ubres (udder)

Las bubis

Las tetas

Las teclas (keys)

Los melones

El teclado (keyboard)

El chicharrón (pork rind)

La pechuga (chicken breast)

Mexislang ways to say testicles

Las albóndigas (the meatballs)

Los blanquillos (the eggs)

Los huevos (also the eggs)

Las bolas (the balls)

Las pelotas (also the balls)

Los huérfanos (the Foster children)

Las talegas

Los tenates

Las verijas.

Mexislang ways to refer to homosexuals

Puñal (short knife, dagger)

Puto

Joto

Maricón

Marica

Tortillas (for lesbians)

Marimacha (for a very masculine woman, or lesbian)

Machorra (same as the previous one)

Del otro bando (from the other team)

Chayote (a mexican vegetable)

Ganso (goose)

Mayate

Cangrejo (crab)

Que camina o le truena la reversa (someone who walks in reverse)

Mexislang ways to say semen

Mecos

Mecánicos

Mecates

La leche (milk)

El *jugo (juice)*

Bajarse por los chescos

To perform oral sex on someone. It literally means, "to go down to pick some sodas".

Ex.

Corté con mi novia, porque no le gustaba bajarse por los chescos.

I broke up with my girlfriend, because she didn't like to blow me.

Un mameluco

A blowjob. Other ways to refer to it are "*mamada*" or "*chupón*". Mameluco actually means baby romper.

Ex.

Abrí la puerta, y vi a Miguel recibiendo un mameluco de un hombre.

I opened the door, and saw Miguel getting a blowjob from a man.

Empiernarse

To spoon someone. It literally means, to get between each other's legs.

Ex.

Cuando hace frío, mi novia y yo When it's cold, I spoon my *nos empiernamos mientras vemos películas.* — girlfriend while we watch movies.

Apapacho

A hug. From it, we get the verb "apapachar" which means to hug. This word actually comes from the Nahuatl verb "pachoa", which means to protect or to cuddle.

Ex.

Me apapachó tan fuerte que me sacó el aire. — He hugged me so hard he took the air out of me.

Pechugona

A woman with big breasts. It's disrespectful for a man to call a woman this way. But if a woman uses this word to describe a fellow gal, there's no problem. It might be even considered a complement. It comes from *pechuga* which means "chicken breast". Other ways to say the same are *chichona*, and *tetona*. The opposite of it is *"plana"* which means a woman with small breasts. It's always disrespectful to call a woman like this.

Ex.

Quisiera ser pechugona como tú. Yo estoy plana. — I wish I had big boobs like you. Mine are really small.

Orto

Anus. Another Mexican slang way to call it is *"el asterisco"* (the asterisk), and *"el ojete"*.

Ex.

Algunos termómetros miden la temperatura del cuerpo por el orto.

Some thermometers measure body temperature from the anus.

Darle vuelo a la hilacha.

Having a lot of love/sexual affairs, may be with a single person, or with different partners.

Ex.

Mi prima le da mucho vuelo a la hilacha. Ya tiene 6 hijos.

My cousin has had a lot of affairs. She already has 6 children.

Jalársela

The action of male masturbation. We have seen the verb jalar previously in this book, but when it is used as a reflexive with the indirect object pronoun of "la" attached to it, it means to jerk off. Sometimes, people tend to say stuff like *"Jalarle el cuello al ganso"* (To pull the neck of a goose), which also means to masturbate.

Ex.

Era adicto a la masturbación, pero no me la he jalado en un mes.

I was addicted to masturbation, but I haven't masturbated for a month.

Manuela

Another way of referring to male masturbation. "Manuela" is actually a female proper name, however, since it's similar to the word *"mano"* (hand), it's also used as a way to refer to fapping. Other ways to say the same thing are *"una chaqueta"*, *"una puñeta"* and *"una paja"*.

Ex.

Puedo no tener novia, pero tengo a manuela.

I may not have a girlfriend, but I can fap.

Ser una nalga

To be a sexual partner in a non-romantic way. It literally means: "to be a buttock". People may also use *"culo"* (ass) instead of *"nalga"*.

Ex.

Estoy enamorada de ti. A él no lo quiero, solo era una nalga.

I'm in love with you. I don't love him, it was purely sexual.

La regla

A woman's period. It can be used as a verb "reglar". It literally means "the rule".

Here there are some other expressions to talk about a girl's period:

- *La marea roja*: The red tide
- *Estar haciendo entomatadas:* To make tortillas with tomato sauce.
- *Tirar aceite:* To leak oil
- *Using the verb "bajar"* (to get down)
- *Estar en sus/esos días.* (to be on her/those days)

Tirar aceite

To accidentally pee in your pants or also, a woman's period. It's very vulgar and disrespectful to say this in front of people who are experiencing this problem.

As said earlier, conjugations of bajar like "*me bajó*", o "*me está bajando*" are used also to refer to a woman's period.

Ex.

¿Por qué no vino tu novia?	Why didn't your girlfriend come?
– No se siente bien, anda tirando aceite.	-She isn't feeling right. She is having her period.

Deslecharse

To ejaculate. People also say "*venirse*", "*irse*" and "*correrse*"

Ex.

No puedes estar embarazada. Siempre me desleché afuera.

You can't be pregnant. I always ejaculated outside.

Tronar el ejote

To lose one's virginity. It literally means to "make the Green bean pop", and it's the equivalent of "popping your cherry".

Ex.

Tiene cuarenta años, y aún no le han tronado el ejote.

She is forty years old, and still hasn't lost her virginity.

Ponedor(a)

A person who really likes sex and has it often. In regular Spanish, being *ponedor*, means to be someone who puts stuff, like money or resources to accomplish a project.

Ex.

Por ser tan ponedoras, mis primas tienen muchos hijos.

My cousins have a lot of children, because they really like to have sex.

Apretada

A woman who doesn't agree to have sex easily. It literally means tight.

Ex.

Ni le hables a esas chavas, son todas bien apretadas. Don't even talk to those girls, you won't take them to bed.

Gordibuena(o)

An attractive chubby woman or man. Of course, for a man, it's completely disrespectful to call a woman this way.

Ex.

Mi novia dejó de ir al gimnasio, y ahora está gordibuena. My girlfriend stopped going to the gym, she' got some pounds on, but she still looks really attractive.

Pedorro

A big ass. You can also say *Culo* and *Botaxis* to refer to ass, but *botaxis* is more used in the South of Mexico. *Pedorro* literally means someone who farts a lot.

Ex.

Esa actriz se operó para tener That actress got surgery to *más grande el pedorro.*   have her ass bigger.

Trapo

A disrespectful way to say someone is a trans person. In regular Spanish, you use this word for a cleaning cloth or rag.

Ex.

Fuimos a un bar gay, y había muchas mujeres atractivas, pero todas eran tortillas o trapos.	We went to a gay bar, and there were many attractive women, but all of them were either lesbians or transsexuals.

Estar Carita

To be a good-looking man. It literally means "to be a little face". People also say, *"estar rostro"*.

Ex.

Tú no sabes lo difícil que es encontrar novia, tú estás carita.	You don't know how hard it is to find a girlfriend, you are good looking.

La jarocha

A clinical operation where a transsexual man removes his reproductive organs to have them shaped like a feminine sexual organ.

Me convertí en transexual cuando me hice la jarocha.	I became a transsexual person when I took the surgery to remove my penis.

Piruja

It can mean a few things, like a very promiscuous woman. A woman who is with a man because of the things he has. It's also a word to refer to a prostitute.

To refer to a promiscuous woman, other mexislang words are: *puta*, *zorra*, and *golfa*.

Ex.

Su marido se escapó con una piruja.	Her husband left and ran away with a whore.

Piropo

A pickup line. In general, *piropos* are compliments and flattery people say to show interest in someone they want to hook up with, and they can be chessy, respectful and /or disrespectful.

Ex.

Mi mejor amiga siempre recibe piropos cuando salimos a pasear.

My best friend always receives flattering comments when we hang out.

Mi Viejo / Vieja

My boyfriend/My husband or My girlfriend/My wife. Some people really like this, some hate it, it depends on the person, but a lot of men use it when their partners aren't around, between male friends, to refer to their girlfriend.

Ex.

Mi vieja es excelente cocinera.   My wife is an excellent cook.

Tener pegue

To have luck and/or skill attracting possible mates. A person "*tiene pegue*" when there's always new people getting interested romantically, and/or sexually in them. It literally means "to have punch".

Ex.

Fui a la fiesta, pero ningún hombre se me acercó. No

I went to the party, but not a single man approached me. I

tengo nada de pegue. can't attract anyone.

Taco de ojo

Eye-candy. To enjoy looking at someone that we find attractive.

Ex.

Me gusta ver el voleibol femenino en las olimpíadas por el taco de ojo.

I like to watch female volleyball on the Olympics because of all the eye-candy.

Aflojar

When a woman finally agrees to have sex with a man. In regular Spanish, *aflojar* means that something that was tight, like a shoe or clothing, it's starting to get loose.

Ex.

Voy a terminar con mi novia, porque han pasado meses y no afloja.

I'm going to break up with my girlfriend, cause months have passed, and she doesn't want to do it with me.

Fajar

To fool around with a partner. It includes kisses, touching and maybe even oral sex but no actual intercourse. The word *agasajo*, or *agasajar*, can be used with this same meaning.

Ex.

Mi novia todavía no afloja, solo hemos llegado a fajar.	My girlfriend hasn't had sex with me, we only kiss and touch each other.

Putero

Brothel or bordello, a place where prostitutes wait to sell their services. Another word for the same thing is *congal* or *casa de citas*.

Also, putero can mean many or a lot of something. Other words and phrases that mean a lot or many in mexican slang are: Chingo, madrazo, chingazo, chinguero, Putazo, Fregazo and friego.

Ex.

Mi hermano se contagió de una venérea por andar yendo a los puteros.	My brother caught an STD because he used to go to the brothels.

Echarse un palo

To have sex. It literally means, to throw yourself a stick. Other verbs used to express the same are: *coger, chingar, joder,* follar.

Ex.

Estaban con prisa de irse. Probablemente van a ir a echarse un palo.	They were in a hurry to leave. They're probably going to have sex.

Chacalón(a)

Someone who dates people way younger than them. Literally, it means "like a jackal".

Ex.

Esa maestra es una chacalona. Uno de sus alumnos es su novio, y es 10 años más joven que ella.	That teacher is like a jackal. One of her students is her boyfriend, and he is 10 years younger than her.

Mayate

A male prostitute. A gay lover or a close friend, implying that you are such good friends, some may think you are a gay couple, even if they know both of you aren't actually gay. This last example, is the most common way it's used, as a friendly tease between male friends.

Ex.

Vente a la reta, tráete a tu mayate. — Come to the match, bring your best friend.

Esos dos hombres son mayates. — Those two men are gay lovers.

Cornudo

Being cheated on. It's the Spanish equivalent of cuckold.

Ex.

La mujer de Miguel y su sancho, lo convirtieron en un cornudo. — Miguel's wife and her lover, made him into a cuckold.

Sancho

When your partner is cheating on you with another person, in Mexican slang, we call this person, the Sancho.

Ex.

Mientras trabajas, el sancho está dándole cariño a tu esposa. — While you are working, the sancho is courting your wife.

Teibol

Strip club. This word comes from the English word "table", because the strippers (*teiboleras*) do their dances on a table.

Ex.

| *Antes de ser bailarina profesional, trabajé como teibolera en un teibol.* | Before I moved on to become a professional dancer, I worked as a stripper at a strip club. |

Ligar

To court, to woo or to hook up.

Ex.

| *Ponte este vestido, y seguro ligas con alguien en la peda.* | If you wear this dress, I'm sure you are going to hook up with someone in the party. |

Estar Bueno(a)

To be sexually attractive, to be hot.

Ex.

| *Está bien bueno ese vato.* | That guy is very hot. |
| *No sé por qué te gusta, ni está* | I don't know why you like her, |

tan buena. she isn't even that hot.

Albur

A pun or a double entendre that usually (but not always) carries sexual undertones. It's usually a clever joke used to disarm you, and give you a spoken punch in the face, while still remaining playful and friendly. It's mostly used between close male friends. However, it's considered rude or distasteful to make puns like this in the presence of a woman or when you are not among friends.

Examples of "albur":

(someone is giving you a beer to hold it for him)

*Agárramela/*Take it.

(Then he grabs his crotch)

*Ésta/*This one.

You can also use *albur* as a verb, "*alburear*", to say you are making a dirty joke at the expense of someone else.

*¿Cómo te llamas?/*What's your name?
Benito Camelo (This name sounds exactly the same as the phrase "Ven y tócamelo" which means "come and touch me").
No se llama así, te está albureando/ That's not his name, he is joking with you.

Hacer de chivo los tamales

To cheat on someone. Literally, it means "to make tamales with goat meat" and the logic behind it is that, usually tamales are made of pork, but sometimes, the cooks cheat and they make tamales out of goat meat instead and without telling anyone.

Ex.

Mientras trabajas, tu esposa te hace de chivo los tamales. — While you work, your wife is cheating on you.

Tirar rollo

To flirt with someone or to communicate using overly complicated language. Someone who does this a lot is called a "rollero". Literally, *tirar* rollo means *"to throw a roll"*.

Ex.

Tuve que tirar un chingo de rollo para terminar mi ensayo. — I had to write a lot of mumbo jumbo to finish the essay.

Deja de tirarle rollo a mi prima. — Stop hitting on my cousin.

Echar los perros

To try to seduce someone without being subtle at all. It literally means "to throw dogs at someone".

Ex.

Deja de echarle los perros a todas, te hace ver desesperado. Stop trying to seduce every girl. It makes you look desperate.

Viejo rabo verde

A perverted old man. A 50 plus man that flirts with young girls.

Ex.

Deja esa muchacha en paz, viejo rabo verde. Podría ser tu hija. Leave that girl alone, you old perv. She could be your daughter.

Mandilón

A man who doesn't take the lead in a relationship, and is always bossed around by his girlfriend or wife. The term comes from the word *mandil* (apron). So, *mandilón* literally means "a man who wears an apron".

Ex.

José nunca viene a los cotorreos. Es bien mandilón, Jose never comes to parties. He is a slave to his wife and he *tiene miedo que su esposa lo regañe.*   doesn't want her to get mad at him.

Panochón

It has two possible meanings depending if it's used on a man or on a woman.

When used on a man, it means coward. It's the Spanish equivalent of being a pussy. People also use the term *puchón* which has the same meaning.

When used on a woman, it's a very unpolite way to express that she's hot. It's almost never used face to face and a man never calls a woman like this directly. It's mainly used by men in social media, hiding behind a computer or between male friends talking about girls.

Panochón comes from the word *panocha* which is another slang term to refer to a woman's genitalia.

Ex.

Ya deja a la enfermera que te inyecte, no seas panochón.   Let the nurse give you a shot already. Don't be such a pussy.

¿Ya viste ese panochón que acaba de cruzar la calle?   Did you see that piece of meat that just crossed the street?

Toloache

Toloache is a love potion made by a girl or a man, in wich they make a dish, or beverage using water that contains fluids from their body, usually boiling some underwear, and then making a dish using that water, with the intention to feed it to a person they want to make fall in love with them. Its also called "*agua de calzón*" (Panties water), and while its not common, sometimes its done by supersticious men or women. In Mexislang, People also use this word a lot, when talking about unlikely couples, saying the one who they consider not worthy of the others affection, used toloache to make the other one fall in love with them.

Ex.

| *Tu novia está muy fea. Creo que te dio toloache.* | Your girlfriend is very ugly. I think she gave you a love potion. |

Encueros

Cuero means leather. To be *Encueros*, or *encuerado*, means to be wearing leather.
This is the slang word used to say you or someone is naked, wearing only your very own human leather. People also say "*estar en pelotas*" to say someone is naked.

Ex.

Fui a una playa nudista, y anduve encuerado todo el día. I went to a nudist beach, and I was naked the whole day.

Cachondo

Slang way to say you are horny or aroused.

Ex.

Esa película tenía escenas que me pusieron cachondo That movie had scenes that made me horny.

Piojito

It literally means a little louse, but in Mexislang, it means to gently play with the hair of your romantic partner, as lice usually are in someones hair.

Ex.

Hazme piojito. Play with my hair.

Hermanos de leche

It literally means "milk brothers" and this is a phrase used to say two people were breast fed by the same woman. In mexican slang, it is something you say when two or more people had sex with the same partners, and they have kind of an unspoken brothership because of that.

Ex.

El pueblo es tan pequeño, que casi todos son hermanos de leche. The town is so small, that almost everyone is having sex with someone other townfolk already had sex with.

Ganado

It literally means livestock. We use "Ganado" for all the potential love interests that are trying to win our affection. Ganado can be just one or also many people. Ex.

El no es muy guapo, pero aun asi tiene ganado. He is not very handsome, but he still has some people interested in him.

Immerse in the language: Some ways to improve your Spanish

One of the many possible reasons people may be interested in this book, may be to learn and understand Spanish better. As someone who has been teaching online for over two years, and has talked and seen methods used by more than 100 students, I decided to write a last chapter with tips and advice to improve your Spanish.

One of the best ways to learn a language is to immerse yourself into it, and for that, you need to recreate the experience of living in a foreign country. Which means that in order to improve, you need to constantly listen, read, write and speak in that language, just like if you were a child learning naturally. Here is a list of some useful resources to study and immerse yourself in Spanish.

1.-**Youtube**: Youtube is filled with many channels that can help you improve, some are directly focused on Spanish learning, like Superholly, Butterfly Spanish, Español Automático, or María Español. Also, there must be a youtuber who speaks Spanish and speaks about things similar to your own interest. You can check out some of these channels, and subscribe to them, and then let the YouTube recommended videos lead you to other Spanish speaking youtubers. This is an easy way to acquire information on topics and things you like, and turn it into learning opportunities. You can also go to the Latin American section of Youtube and see what´s trending, listen to some music in Spanish, or whatever viral Spanish video in Spanish that catches your attention.

2.- **Netflix**. There is a Netflix hack very useful for language learners. First, you need to make a new profile in your Netflix account, and then, go into your settings. There you can change the language of that whole profile, and access Latin American Spanish, as well as Spanish from Spain, and watch or rewatch all of your favorite shows, while you learn Spanish. This trick works for every language, so if you are learning multiple ones, or are interested in a language that isn't Spanish, you can also use this trick.

3.- **Italki**: This is the website I use to teach Spanish online in the comfort of my home. This site is a big community of language learners as well as a marketplace for people willing to teach a language for a few dollars. Registration is free, and you can ask questions, read articles, write entries so people correct them, or make language exchanges if people are willing to. Also, there are a lot of professional teachers and informal tutors in every language, and every teacher has their own schedule, teaching style and price, so you can search for one who suits your needs. If you make your account using my referral link, and then make at least one purchase of a lesson, you'll get 10 extra dollars to try out the site a little, as well as 10 for me, that are only usable to buy lessons, which is great because I have always wanted to learn some Japanese. I'll leave my referral link here: https://www.italki.com/i/BH0CAB?hl=es

4.-**Reddit**: There are language learning subreddits for every language, and there is a few that are Spanish specific. There you can ask for advice, questions, and also, share and get learning resources, like free books, verb lists, flashcards, etc.

You can also look for language practice, and language exchange subreddits, if you want to practice talking for free, it's totally doable, but it will need some time and effort to find a partner who can adjust to your time, and needs.

5.-**Anki and Memrise**: Flashcard apps made for studying different topics, and some of these topics are of course, languages. This is a way to memorize words and phrases by making that process easier and less boring. You can download them for Windows, Android, IOS, and MAC versions of these apps, and also prebuild decks of flashcards of different topics, as well as the ability to make your own decks.

6.- **Fluent forever**: This is a book that instead of teaching you Spanish, it teaches you a method to learn languages efficiently and fast, focusing on pronunciation, and with a lot of memory techniques and tips for you to improve your success at learning. I have noticed how people who use this method learn faster. Besides the book, it has a paid premium program and an upcoming app that seems to be an improved version of anki, so if you are interested, you may check their page.

7.- **Fluentu**: Fluentu is a monthly subscription program that teaches you languages via immersion with videos spoken by native speakers. It has multiple languages beside Spanish, and it has a free trial for you to check it out before you buy it.

8.- **Spanishpod 101**: This is a podcast in Spanish, but it also has, depending on your subscription, a handful of resources for you to study and learn the language, with tons of lessons, transcripts and free videos and audio files about Spanish learning.

9.- **Duolingo**: Duolingo is a very popular website/app that teaches you language basics, with an easy to use, and very visual interface, that gamifies the learning (it gives you experience points and level progression almost like a videogame), and makes the user more motivated to learn. It may not be real traditional lessons, but it's still a great tool for people starting to learn languages.

10.- **Hellotalk**: Finding someone to practice the language you are studying is hard for some people, but Hellotalk was made to solve this problem. This is an app to find people to exchange languages, but it's easy to use, and its interface is similar to modern social networks. If you are targeting a single language, the app is free, but if you want to target more than one at the same time, you'll have to pay a small fee.